Richard !
Job

Bob Royall *2 Peter 1:3*
Bob Royall

SPIRITUAL LEADERSHIP COACHING

CONNECTING PEOPLE TO GOD'S HEART AND PURPOSES

A book for anyone who wants to improve at spiritually influencing others

Dr. Richard Blackaby & Dr. Bob Royall
with Brett Pyle

Blackaby Ministries International
Jonesboro, Georgia

SPIRITUAL LEADERSHIP COACHING: CONNECTING PEOPLE
TO GOD'S HEART AND PURPOSES
PUBLISHED BY BLACKABY MINISTRIES INTERNATIONAL
P.O. Box 1035
Jonesboro, GA 30237
www.blackaby.org

Unless otherwise noted, all Scripture quotations are taken from the Christian Standard Bible®, Copyright © 2017 by Holman Bible Publishers. Used by permission. Christian Standard Bible® and CSB® are federally registered trademarks of Holman Bible Publishers.

ISBN 978-0-692-93900-0

Publisher's Cataloging-in-Publication data

Names: Blackaby, Richard, 1961-, author. | Royall, Bob, author. | Pyle, Brett, author.
Title: Spiritual leadership coaching : connecting people to God's heart and purposes / Dr. Richard Blackaby & Dr. Bob Royall with Brett Pyle.
Description: Includes bibliographical references. | Jonesboro, GA: Blackaby Ministries, 2018.
Identifiers: ISBN 978-0-692-93900-0 | LCCN 2018943504
Subjects: LCSH Leadership. | Christian life. | Church work. | Personal coaching. | Christian leadership. | BISAC RELIGION / Christian Church / Leadership | RELIGION / Christian Life / Personal Growth | BUSINESS & ECONOMICS / Mentoring & Coaching
Classification: LCC BV652.1 .B62 2018 | DDC 253--dc23

Printed in the United States of America
2018 -- 1st ed.

Contents

Preface ix

Foreward xiii

A Leadership Tale xix

*Introduc*tion xxiii

Section One: The Heart of Spiritual Leadership Coaching 1

   1. What is Spiritual Leadership Coaching? 3

   2. Character Counts 21

   3. The Underlying Core 27

   4. The Bible and Coaching 39

   5. Prayer and God's Agenda 49

Section Two: Relationship-Building Skills 59

   6. Establishing Trust 63

   7. Being Spiritually Present 71

   8. Active Multi-Level Listening 85

Section Three: Awareness-Raising Skills 97

   9. Expanding Awareness 101

   10. Powerful Spirit-led Questions 113

   11. Concise Messages 127

Section Four: Focusing and Commitment Skills 137

   12. Narrowing the Focus 141

   13. Calling for Commitment 151

   14. Chosen Accountability 159

Section Five: Futuring Skills 175

  15. Envisioning a God-Inspired Future 179

  16. Anticipating and Overcoming Obstacles 187

  17. Mining for Takeaways 195

Section Six: Putting it All to Work 207

  18. Coaching through Pain 209

  19. Coaching People through the Seasons

     of Life 229

  20. Six Necessary Comforts for Effective

     Spiritual Coaching 243

  21 Ten Pitfalls Coaches Must Avoid 253

Conclusion 263

About the Authors 265

Spiritual Leadership Coaching Workshop 267

Become a Blackaby-Certified Coach 269

Other Blackaby Ministries Resources 275

ACKNOWLEDGMENTS

We are indebted to the following master coaches who provided valuable input which informed coaching aspects of this book:

- Jane Creswell, MCC, Partner GetPositive.Today
- Linda Miller, MCC, Global Liaison for Coaching, The Ken Blanchard Companies
- Sara Smith, MCC, CEO, Smith Leadership

We would also like to express our sincere gratitude for the following readers who also provided very helpful feedback on our manuscript: Craig Faubel, PCC, Dr. Bruce Aubrey, Greg Herring, Latrecia Raffety, Verna Verity, Dr. Teresa Royall, Rev. Steve Ford, David Drawdy, Richard Rock, and Carolyn Hannah.

We are also very grateful for the fantastic team at Blackaby Ministries who contributed to the success of this book. Carrie Blackaby's careful and insightful editing brought our message to greater clarity and impact. Sarah Blackaby's artistic talents are apparent on the cover. Steve Parsons formatted the collections of chapters into proper format for publishing. Rick Fisher and Sam Camp each contributed their energies to ensure the success of this project. Great job BMI team! We could not have done it without your able assistance!

PREFACE

Is this book for me?

This book is for anyone who desires to improve their spiritual influence with other people through spiritual coaching skills. Who might that include?

- Career coaches who wish to learn new ways to bring God into a conversation in an authentic and transformative way.
- Pastors who long to have a deeper, more profound spiritual impact on those in their congregation and community.
- Executives who need new ideas for bringing out the best in their employees.
- Educators who want to empower students (and their mentors) to use effective coaching skills for spiritual transformation.
- Parents seeking new ways to communicate with their children so they can positively shape both their behavior and their heart.
- Small group leaders and members who desire to develop the necessary skills to help each other grow in Christlikeness.

In this book, you will notice terms such as coach, spiritual coach, leadership coach, and spiritual leadership coach. We use these terms somewhat interchangeably to refer to someone who employs the skills we highlight in this book. We did not write this book exclusively for a few highly trained individuals. Rather, it describes anyone— such as those mentioned above—who engages in the practices we describe. We hope that, as you read this book, God shapes you into a spiritual leadership coach He will use for His glory. Some readers will gain important insights that are immediately applicable. Others will want to learn more by attending one of our coaching workshops.[1] A few of you may become so interested in learning these skills that you begin the process to become a Blackaby-certified spiritual leadership coach. More information concerning these options is available at the back of the book.

This book is a collaboration among friends who share a passion for shaping spiritual leaders from the brittle and lumpy clay of humanity. Within these pages, you will learn the following:

- How the Seven Realities of Experiencing God provides a spiritual framework for coaching.
- Four levels of listening and why each is important.
- The power of a Spirit-led question to open hearts and minds.
- When to speak a hard truth into someone's life.
- Ways to incorporate Scripture into conversations without coming across as preachy or pushy.
- How to move conversations from meandering to meaningful.
- New ways to move from good intentions to clear commitments.

---

[1]For more about our Spiritual Leadership Coaching Workshop, go to www.blackabycoaching.org/workshop.

- How painful experiences can become a springboard to true spiritual breakthroughs.
- How to help people successfully navigate the seasons of their life.

Join us for the adventure of a lifetime, shaping people through spiritual leadership coaching!

FOREWORD

"Someone needs to write Experiencing God: Coach Edition!"

I wrote that sentence in the margin of page 71 in my copy of *Experiencing God* by Henry T. Blackaby and Claude V. King just before June 14, 1999.

I know that date because I was studying *Experiencing God* with my friend and Christian coaching colleague Linda Miller who lived in Seattle. I was in Raleigh, so we met via phone every other week to share our learning. I put the dates of those calls at the top of each chapter so I would be prepared for our discussions.

And now, it seems, to tell you.

We marveled at the book's relevance to our coaching journey. We spent six months walking intentionally through each chapter together, squeezing out every possible bit of wisdom.

My friend Bob Royall emailed recently saying he and Richard Blackaby had written a book, and he asked if I would mind reading it. As I poured over each page, I remembered what I wrote in the margin of *Experiencing God* almost nine years ago. I'm delighted to say somebody wrote the book! And it's much better than I imagined.

The book you are now reading, the one I longed for, is as needed today as it was then.

Why did I think we needed a Coach Edition of *Experiencing God?*

I noticed that *all* the coaching I was doing, with believers and pre-believers alike, seemed to fit somewhere into the Seven Realities of *Experiencing God*. My mindset as a Christian coach, my skills and competencies, and the ways I watched God at work in coaching conversations were all described at some level in *Experiencing God*.

And yet, Linda and I still had to do some "translating" from the book's vocabulary to the vocabulary of Christian coaching, which was just emerging in 1999. The margins of my copy are populated with those "translations." At the end of every chapter, I wrote a list of behaviors that distinguish a Christian coach from other coaches. Most of those notes were revelations that came as I read with relatively new coach eyes. I was thirsty to connect my faith with my new role as a coach, and *Experiencing God* became that connection for me. I am forever grateful that God orchestrated the timing of all that.

Thanks to Bob and Richard, you'll have a much easier time of it. They've done the translation for you and established the connection between Christian coaching and *Experiencing God* in spiritual leadership coaching.

The years of 1997-2001 were formative for me as a coach. I started my coach training in 1997, and within 30 days I joined the International Coach Federation, hired my first coach, and started coaching my first client—the woman who sat beside me at church choir. By June 1998, I became the first internal coach at IBM.

Internal coaching was just beginning then. The first book on Christian coaching wasn't released until

2001. There was so much I didn't know at that time. I didn't know that I would later be known for creating a coaching culture at IBM and several other large companies. I didn't know my first presentation at an ICF conference in October of 1999 would create such buzz about internal coaching that *Newsday Press, Investors Business Daily, HR Magazine,* and *TIME* would write articles about it. I didn't know organizations I coached would win the ICF Prism Award for achieving the best business results through coaching. I didn't know I would be an inaugural recipient of the ICF Midwest Thomas Leonard Achievement Award for coaching innovation. I didn't know I would eventually author a couple of books on coaching and co-author several ICF-approved coach training programs.

And most significantly, I didn't know that I would eventually see signs of God at work in *every single person* I coached for the next 20 years.

What I knew was that God called me to be a missionary to the corporate world. *Experiencing God* gave me the confidence I needed to persevere in the work God designed for me. All of this God-activity emerged from the spiritual marker of our study between March and September of 1999.

Now, there are more than 100 books that refer to Christian coaching. So do we actually need another one? If so, why? When Bob asked me to read this book, I asked myself those questions. I mean, is there anything left to say about Christian coaching?

First, we need this book because of who the authors are. I first connected with Bob Royall at Christian coach training sessions at a North Carolina retreat center. He was then the director of the Doctor of Ministry Program at a seminary and was looking into coaching as a practical tool for ministry leaders. My husband and I became friends with Bob and Teresa over the years and were so excited to learn that he was leading the initiative to incorporate coaching and coach training into Blackaby Ministries. Bob is a thoughtful, knowledgeable, Holy Spirit-led, practical, theological scholar. I learned as much from Bob challenging me in coach training classes as he learned from me, I'm sure.

I've yet to meet Richard personally, but I have met his father, Henry. I had the privilege of having an hour-long conversation with him in the greenroom at a *Lead Like Jesus Encounter* event. He sat by himself, reading his Bible prior to giving his keynote presentation. When I saw this hero of my faith journey, I felt compelled to speak with him. Henry graciously invited me to sit and chat. The conversation was free and easy, as though we had known each other for years. His margin-note-filled Bible was open to a passage he would share in his keynote. I'm a Bible-margin-note-taker too and asked if I could browse through his Bible. What an experience to read a few of his notes, hear some of his explanations, and see a precious picture he had tucked inside depicting himself as an 11 year-old walking hand-in-hand down a sidewalk with his father! He explained that he felt like he was on top of the world getting to spend that day with his father and that he tried to give that kind of special, undivided attention to his children, including Richard.

Seeing no space left in the Bible's margins, I asked what he planned to do. He said, simply, "I'll get another Bible. And soon I'll have enough of these to give to each of my children." I made plans to do the same. So, I knew I would be inspired by a book Henry's son and now leader of Blackaby Ministries wrote. True to form, my frequent notes in the margins of the pre-publication version of this book are a testament to the newness it introduces.

Second, this book offers practical guidance on how to stay focused on the mission to help people connect (or reconnect) to God and fully embrace their authentic God-given identity. This book is the intersection of the Seven Realities of *Experiencing God*, Christian coaching, Scripture, and prayer. No additional translation required. It's all right here.

It delivers as a great resource for people who want to improve their ability to spiritually influence others. The Biblical basis expressed throughout the book for coaching relationships is more thorough than in other Christian coaching resources. Bob and Richard do more than just write about coaching. They offer examples to demonstrate how spiritual leadership coaching sounds in sample questions and dialogues.

Third, this book is packed with ideas that are unique to spiritual leadership coaching. I am pleased with the freshness they bring to the arena of Christian coaching.

Most challenging to me personally was their suggestion that each Christian coach apply their professional coach level of listening to the way they listen to the Lord. It caused me to wonder, "What if I listen to the Lord as intently as I listen to clients?" This concept transformed me, and it is only one example of many.

Finally, you'll find a unique perspective on accountability that is congruent with ICF standards and grounded in biblical principles. One of my favorite chapters is about coaching through changing seasons, again, new insights for Christian coaches.

I could continue raving about this book, but you're just going to have to read it for yourself. I will ask any coach who works with us at GetPositive.Today to read this book. We'll study it together, discuss it, and incorporate these new concepts into the way we coach Christian business leaders to live their faith.

Thank you Bob and Richard for following God's call to publish this book. And may God bless your ministry as you continue to pursue God-sized goals.

Jane Creswell, Master Certified Coach
Partner, GetPositive.Today
Author, *Christ-Centered Coaching: 7 Benefits for Ministry Leaders*,
The Complete Idiot's Guide to Coaching for Excellence

A LEADERSHIP TALE

CLIFF was a pastor with a good heart and great intentions, but on certain days, Mondays especially, he was usually ready to throw in the spiritual towel. Despite his efforts to preach biblically, to pray earnestly, and to visit his members diligently, he saw little genuine change in his people. Initiatives he took with the staff and lay leaders often resulted in half-hearted semi-compliance that went nowhere.

Come to think of it, his dismal progress at work reminded him of his EFFORTS AT HOME WITH HIS KIDS, EMILY AND ZACK. He wanted the best for them, but they didn't see it that way. Dad's agenda was low on their priority list, and he was tired of pushing them to achieve their best. Pastor Cliff knew that being the preacher's kids was difficult. Everyone in the congregation felt it was their responsibility to observe his children, and they were quick to point out their lapses. But he, too, had expectations for them. Too high, perhaps. He had lost count of the times he had come on too strong with them.

One Sunday, an EXECUTIVE named MARK joined the congregation along with his family. Cliff immediately noticed something different about him. Over time, Mark became more than merely another church member to Cliff. Mark confided that he felt called to be a Barnabas to him, a trusted friend who could bring out the best in Pastor Cliff. Over occasional lunches, Mark would listen intently as Cliff poured out his hopes and frustrations, then he would ask perceptive questions that allowed Cliff to see his ministry, and even his role as a father, in an entirely new light.

Pastor Cliff greatly respected Mark and looked forward to their talks. He wished he could be more like him and he told him so one day.

To his surprise, Mark rebuffed him. "You don't want to be like me, especially the guy I used to be," Mark said. "Years ago, I was stuck like you, constantly pushing my employees. I wanted to reach the top and was a hard charger. Annual evaluations of employees were a bloodbath as I pointed out mistakes and prodded them to achieve an ever higher output.

"Then my own time of reckoning arrived. Upper management noticed the decreasing output and frequent turnover in my department. To reverse the trend, they did a 360 evaluation on me. The results were not good. They were downright devastating! I was shocked to learn that on all three levels—supervisors, peers, and reports—I was viewed as an ineffective leader.

"They brought in an EXECUTIVE COACH, Jackson, who I expected would ream me out and push a remedial 'development plan' on me. But he didn't. Instead, he got to know me and learned what I wanted out of my life, career, and family. He probed deeper to discover my core values. When I sheepishly told him I was a Christian, he told me he saw his work as a calling from God. His mission was to bring out God's best in his clients, myself included.

"Jackson taught me so much. More than I could ever say. I am a far better leader because of him: more compassionate, insightful, and effective. That year of coaching with Jackson transformed my career and eventually led me to achieve my dream—I became the CEO of the very company that conducted the infamous 360 evaluation on me!"

Cliff continued to learn from his friend Mark, who helped him see beyond his own perspective and listen on a deeper, more empathetic level to those he encountered. Though difficult at first, Cliff discovered he did not need to have "the answer" to everyone's queries. He learned to ask more questions. He also started looking for places God was working around him. To his great surprise, Pastor Cliff noticed the relational walls between him and others slowly coming down. When he shared ideas and provided guidance, he was better received. The staff began to function more cohesively, and staff members were more eager to share ideas for improving the church's ministries.

Looking back a year later, Pastor Cliff marveled at how much his life had improved. He had assumed the people he led were the problem. He learned that, by changing his approach and developing new skills, people responded much more positively to his leadership. Leading finally became exciting and fulfilling.

As you read this brief vignette, you may have recognized yourself in the story. Perhaps you struggle, as Cliff did, to bring out the best in people. You may see ways your own "standard operating system" with others is ineffective. Are you open to considering a new approach to influencing others, one that honors the image of God each person carries, and attend to ways God is shaping them for His glory? If so, read on . . .

INTRODUCTION
by Richard Blackaby

I have to make a confession. I sometimes talk too much. Okay, I often talk too much. And I'm not just referring to the times my sweet wife, Lisa, gives me a look at parties that says, "Perhaps you should try this delicious spinach dip and let someone else speak for a while." I'm also not suggesting that I should *never* talk, although I have been convicted by Proverbs 17:28: *"Even a fool is considered wise when he keeps silent . . ."* Rather, I realize I speak too much when people ask for advice.

I am a speaker and author, so communication is my livelihood. I am passionate about helping Christian leaders. Pastors regularly take me to restaurants so they can bend my ear about a leadership challenge they are facing. I was in my restaurant counseling role when I first noticed my problem.

A troubled pastor bared his soul to me about a difficulty he was having in his church. Having dealt with many similar issues and knowing the restaurant was closing in less than an hour, I responded by spewing forth as much wisdom as I could. The restaurant manager eventually approached our table and diplomatically informed us that the restaurant had closed fifteen minutes earlier.

As the pastor and I parted ways, I wondered if anything I said would make a difference in his life. Knowing that truth sets people free, I had tried to set as much truth before the hurting man as possible (John 8:32). But therein, I realized, was my problem. I was trying to find a solution rather than helping the pastor discover God's answer. I was talking so much the person could not hear his own voice, let alone God's. I had tried to be profound, yet nothing is as earth-shattering as a word from God.

Ultimately, I had focused on making memorable statements rather than asking soul-searching questions. By uttering opinions, I was setting myself up to be the hero. Had I listened better and asked more perceptive questions, the man would have discovered a truth from God that could set him free.

Blackaby Ministries International has developed a spiritual leadership coaching ministry that is different from most other coaching services. We do not ask the question, "Where do you want to go with your life?" Instead, we ask, "Where do you sense God wants to take you?" Our goal is not to help people experience their dreams, but to enable them to embrace God's will. Our coaches seek to withdraw into the background during the discussion so the Holy Spirit can assume center stage. We understand that giving people a solution is not as impactful as helping them discover God's answer.

In my own journey as a coach, I have found that stating an opinion is easier than asking a probing question. I have also learned that I do not need to match my clients' experiences with my own. My relevancy comes from actively and compassionately listening.

Finally, I have learned that most people could benefit from meeting with a leadership coach. Everyone falls into ruts, slides into ineffective routines, and makes false assumptions. Everyone has blind spots. Everyone has room for improvement.

Spiritual leadership coaches help people view themselves and their circumstances more clearly. They also wisely refrain from taking God's place in people's lives. Instead, they skillfully and adeptly lead their clients into God's presence so they can hear His thoughts for themselves.

Spiritual leadership coaches are not just for C-Suite executives.[1] Many parents today are failing with their children yet falsely assume they cannot do anything about it. Church leaders are quick to blame Satan and spiritual warfare for their lack of success when the real culprit may be their poor leadership skills. God has a purpose for every person. Coaches help people discover and embrace that purpose.

Every year, Blackaby Ministries International provides workshops for men and women who want to develop their coaching skills. Some of the participants intend to become professional coaches, while others simply want to become better pastors, volunteers, or parents. People have traveled from numerous states, Canada, France, Nigeria, Togo, South Africa, Honduras, and the Philippines to attend. The material we teach in those workshops has received such a positive response that we felt compelled to put it into writing.

---

[1] A C-Suite executive is a key leader in an organization, filling such roles as CEO (Chief Executive Officer), COO (Chief Operational Officer), CFO (Chief Financial Officer), etc.

Coaches who have been trained in mainstream coaching programs may be concerned about our method. We approach coaching from a biblically informed viewpoint, convinced that God is actively at work in and around each person. While coaches don't experience God *for* their clients, they do invite His presence and purpose to be made known *within* the coaching conversation. Other people may wonder if using coaching skills is too person-centered, worldly, or relativistic. They may feel more comfortable preaching or teaching the Bible. We encourage people to view a coach approach not as a replacement for these valuable methods but as an additional tool in their discipleship toolbox. Jesus demonstrated that a well-placed, Spirit-led question is vastly more powerful than a torrent of words. The Bible records Jesus asking 339 questions![2]

Not all words are equally powerful. Some have little effect on people. Others are life-changing. In these troubled days, people need their words to make an eternal difference. We hope that this book inspires and equips you to exert a positive and decisive impact on others.

---

[2]Go to http://339questionsjesusasked.com/english/ to obtain a free copy of Bob Tiede's ebook *339 Questions Jesus Asked*.

The Heart of Spiritual Leadership Coaching

CHAPTER 1

What is Spiritual Leadership Coaching?

All our knowledge has its origins in our perceptions.
Leonardo da Vinci

*The voyage of discovery is not in seeking new
landscapes but in having new 'eyes.'*
Marcel Proust

You have heard that it was said . . . But I tell you . . .
Jesus
(Matthew 5:21-22, 27-28, 31-32, 33-34, 38-39, 43-44)

Two years ago, I (Richard) made a bold resolution: I was finally going to master golf. I had attempted to learn several times before. Periodically, I would play a round with well-intentioned friends who patiently offered advice on how to improve my game. "Bend your head this way . . . grip your driver this way . . . lean here . . . look there . . . stand here . . . tilt that way . . ." Piloting a 747 through takeoff would seemingly require fewer check lists than taking one swing with my driver.

Finally, I decided to enlist professional help. My golf coach told me to take a swing while he filmed me. I frantically tried to recall the advice my friends had given me through the years. By the time I bent, stiffened, positioned, and gripped the way I had learned, I was so contorted I looked like I was playing "Twister" rather than driving a golf ball. The instructor immediately gave me some crucial advice: *Forget everything I knew.* Much of what my friends told me was incorrect. Some of their tips were actually incompatible with other advice I had received. I had to start over. In the process, I discovered that unlearning can be more challenging than learning!

Many people hold presuppositions about leadership coaching that are incorrect or unhelpful. They might inaccurately assume coaching is identical to giving advice, consulting, or counseling. To become an effective coach, therefore, it is essential to understand what spiritual leadership coaching is and what it is not.

SPIRITUAL LEADERSHIP COACHING IS NOT:

1. Counseling

Troubled people might enlist a counselor to solve a psychological or interpersonal problem. A student I (Bob) encountered while ministering among college students in the Pacific Northwest clearly showed me the value of this respectable profession.

Vince (name has been changed) introduced himself to me as a spiritual seeker desiring salvation. As a young collegiate minister, I was overjoyed to lead him to embrace Jesus as his Lord and Savior. The next time I saw Vince, however, he was still seeking salvation! In fact, he sought a new salvation experience every time I saw him. I finally asked him how many times he had prayed a sinner's prayer. "Hundreds of times," he admitted.

Vince suffered from a psychological malady that prevented him from accepting God's spiritual solution to his angst. He retained an abiding sense of impurity no teaching or rational arguments could resolve. He needed a Christian psychologist who understood his illness and the ways of God.

Counselors are trained to diagnose and treat emotional, psychological, and interpersonal problems. Coaches, on the other hand, allow clients to make their own decisions. They do not view their clients as sick souls needing to be fixed. Rather, they work with clients who are healthy and capable enough to make wise choices and follow through with their commitments.

2. Consulting

Church and business leaders are familiar with consultants. Traditionally, consultants arrive from out of town and pull official-looking files out of their leather briefcase. The leader presents a problem, and the consultant—a recognized expert—provides a solution. For example, a pastor might employ a church growth consultant to study his church and offer recommendations for change. This practice can produce positive results. But consultants may also leave people feeling stupid or misunderstood. The pastor might think, "Wow, that guy knows his stuff! If I were as smart as he is, I could build a big church like he did!" Or he may grouse, "That guy doesn't really understand my church! I bet he gives the same advice to all his clients!" In either case, the focus remains on the consultant's knowledge.

Expert consultants have their place, but human understanding is limited. Few military experts would have advised Gideon to leave most of his soldiers behind before engaging in a battle. Had a military consultant told Joshua to march around Jericho seven times before blowing trumpets, he would have been drummed out of the armed forces! But in both situations, God desired to demonstrate His power in a manner that defied common wisdom and brought Him maximum glory.

Relying too heavily on consultants can be problematic, as people may depend on their consultant rather than on God. Each time they face a problem, they might summon their consultant to provide yet another solution. Coaches, by contrast, help people find God's solution for their problem. Coaching is not meant to foster long-term dependence on others. Rather, it is designed to help people develop healthy processes for discovering and implementing God's will.

3. Discipleship

Christians, especially church leaders, naturally gravitate toward biblical rather than secular language.

While the term "leadership coaching" is not found in the Bible, the command to make disciples is. True discipleship, practiced in the manner of Jesus, does more than immerse people in Christian teaching. It develops spiritual leaders. Nevertheless, spiritual leadership coaching is not identical to discipleship. Typical leadership coaching focuses on specific areas people seek to improve or problems they wish to solve. Discipleship is a broader effort that covers the gamut of Christian teaching and practices.

4. Mentoring

People who wish to gain expertise in a particular field may pursue a mentor. In such relationships, mentors do the bulk of the talking as they share their experiences and wisdom with the person they are mentoring. In a spiritual leadership coaching relationship, coaches ask more questions and tell fewer stories than mentors typically do. Coaching clients attempt to gain wisdom from God's activity in their own life. They are responsible for identifying which problem they want to address and the most appropriate method to use. In this approach, God is the expert, not the coach.

5. Supervision

At times, supervisors utilize coaching techniques to enhance their employees' performance. While their primary motivation is typically to increase productivity, this technique also enables those they supervise to develop knowledge and skills. Utilizing coaching techniques for this endeavor is certainly superior to the classic "command and control" approach to management, and it can produce admirable results.

One of the challenges of combining leadership coaching with supervision, however, is that employees keenly feel the power differential between themselves and their manager. This inequality inhibits honesty and vulnerability when employees fear negative information might affect their job status. Supervisors, therefore, must create tangible assurances of safety when coaching employees.

Another challenge of this method is that remedial coaching imposed on a reluctant subject rarely effects positive change, because it does not tap into the person's intrinsic motivations (see Chapter 14). Therefore, while supervisors can certainly use coaching skills in their work, they are not always ideal coaches.

WHAT *IS* SPIRITUAL LEADERSHIP COACHING?

When seeking to understand spiritual leadership coaching, it can be helpful to consider how respected coaching organizations define it. The International Coach Federation (ICF) is the leading global professional coaching organization, known for setting high professional standards, providing independent certification, and building a network of credentialed coaches.[1] The ICF is a broad group of executive, life, and career coaches who hold a wide variety of religious perspectives. The following definition of coaching

---

[1] See the www.coachfederation.org website organizational description.

reflects the diversity of the group's coaches while also highlighting coaching's most common processes.

ICF Definition of Coaching

> **Partnering with clients in a thought-provoking and creative process that inspires them to maximize their personal and professional potential.**

These are some strengths of this definition:

- First, it recognizes that coaching is a partnership rather than an imparting relationship. Coach and coachee work together to realize the coachee's potential.
- Second, it speaks ably of the creative and provocative relationship that exists between the two parties.
- Third, it recognizes that coaching is typically an ongoing process. Rarely does coaching achieve significant results in a single encounter.
- Finally, it highlights the fact that coaching is designed to develop the coachee's potential.

What is missing? While this definition fits the ICF's diverse member base, it leaves out several important aspects of Christ-centered, biblical coaching. Here are a few of those missing elements:

- *God as the primary party in a coaching relationship.* A Christian coach understands that

God is not silent or passive in a person's life. God, like His Word, *"is living and active. Sharper than any double-edged sword, [He] penetrates even to dividing soul and spirit, joints and marrow; [He] judges the thoughts and attitudes of the heart"* (Heb. 4:12).

- *A shared understanding of God.* A Christian coach can certainly coach a non-Christian. The coaching experience works best, however, when both parties hold the same basic assumptions about God and His methods. Because the ICF includes both devout Christians and atheists, its underlying assumptions are vague. Spiritual leadership coaching is rooted in the understanding that God, as revealed in the Bible, is the ultimate authority, not the coach or the client.

- *Self-actualization is not the goal.* Human history is littered with the consequences of pursuing self-interest above all else. Self-centeredness and pride stand at the heart of what the Bible calls sin. Human beings were not created to achieve their own dreams but to reflect God's glory by fulfilling His purposes. Spiritual leadership coaching, therefore, is a God-oriented approach to coaching in which people, with a coach's guidance, come to understand, embrace, and live out God's unique purpose for their life. Christians recognize, as the *Second Westminster Confession* declares, that the chief end in man is not self-actualization but to glorify God and enjoy Him forever.

To glorify God, people must seek His will and purposes in all they do. At this point, our definition builds on the ICF definition and incorporates our unique focus.

Our Definition of Spiritual Leadership Coaching

> **Spirit-led use of prayer, Scripture, and coaching skills to invite awareness of the activity of God and to help people align their life, and those they lead, with God's purposes.**

This definition acknowledges that God is at work in and around each person being coached. It recognizes that the Holy Spirit works through prayer, Scripture, and coaching to enable people to recognize God's activity in their life and to join Him in it.

POSITIVE ASSUMPTIONS

To understand spiritual leadership coaching better, let's begin with some positive assumptions.

First, the spiritual leadership coaching approach assumes clients are created in God's image and are emotionally and spiritually *healthy* enough to connect with and follow Him. If they are not emotionally healthy and spiritually motivated, coaching may not be the best way to help them. Of course, no one is perfect, and levels of spiritual health vary. But coaches should ask themselves this question: Am I building on the islands of health within people's soul or do I see them as a problem to fix?

Second, this approach assumes people are capable. Everyone has abilities that can be honed, enhanced, and focused. But for coaching to be successful, people must be capable of building on insights they gain through coaching.

Third, it assumes the people being coached are *responsible.* Once they make commitments to themselves, God, and the coach, they will normally follow through with their resolve.

Instead of viewing them as ignorant souls who need to be educated or "fixed," skilled coaches build on their clients' existing capabilities. People may occasionally fail to fully live up to these assumptions, but a coach can help clients grow toward them.

As a result of these underlying assumptions, a coach approach to spiritual leadership includes these characteristics:

- *Collaborative.* The coach and coachee seek the Lord and His solutions together.
- *Person-Centered.* Coaches focus on people, not just problems. They help clients find God's solutions to their challenges. Because each person has infinite God-given worth, coaches do not disparage people while addressing their problems. Coaches begin by acknowledging where people are, rather than

where they think they should be. They focus on personal growth and self-mastery.

- *Discovery-Based.* Self-discovery is more meaningful than hand-me-down insights from another person. An effective coach, like a trusted guide, leads clients on a journey of personal and spiritual discovery. Each session is an opportunity to gain new insights about God and His purposes. At the same time, the word discovery fails to capture the full sense of what happens during coaching, because spiritual truth cannot simply be discovered. God must reveal it. Jesus' prayer to the Father in Matthew 11:25 acknowledges this truth:

> "At that time Jesus said, 'I praise you, Father, Lord of heaven and earth, because you have hidden these things from the wise and learned, and revealed them to little children.'"

Scripture also asserts that people can find God: *"You will seek Me and find Me when you search for Me with all your heart"* (Jer. 29:13). Coaches encourage their clients to prepare their hearts and minds for God's revelation.

- *Involves Actionable Steps.* Eventually, insights should motivate actions of faith. One of the greatest rewards of coaching is helping people take specific steps forward. Coaches guide people to evaluate and choose actions that align with God's will.
- *Effective.* Research demonstrates that people typically retain only 20-40% of what they learn

at training events. But when training workshops are paired with personalized coaching, long-term learning and skill acquisition increases to about 75%! Consider the enormous amount of teaching and preaching the average Christian ingests weekly. Unfortunately, a large gap typically exists between what Christians know they should do and what they actually practice. Most people can identify certain actions that would improve their life and leadership skills, but they often fail to take them. Personalized coaching helps people translate good intentions into actionable steps.

Effective spiritual leadership coaches require certain skill sets. We will overview twelve essential coaching skills in subsequent chapters. But skills alone are not enough. Coaches also need to have a proper mindset. Letting go of the compulsion to answer questions, wise coaches understand the power of attentive listening and Spirit-led questions. For some, refraining from giving answers requires a radical departure from their natural tendencies.

THE INTERPLAY BETWEEN COACHING, SCRIPTURE, PRAYER, AND THE SEVEN REALITIES

Spiritual leadership coaching consists of three essential aspects. The diagram below illustrates these crucial elements:

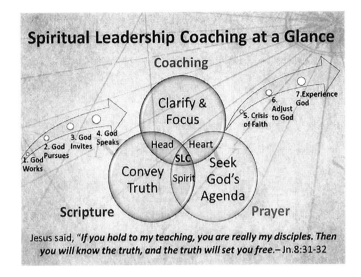

First, notice the three circles in the diagram:

- **Prayer:** Coaches help people find God's agenda through intercession and guided prayer.
- **Scripture:** Coaches draw out ways God's revealed truth applies to the situation.
- **Coaching:** Coaches utilize coaching techniques to enhance clarity and focus, which leads to action.

Each of these circles, operating in harmony, reveals God's purposes in a person's life. When one element is missing, coaching is incomplete:

- Coaching coupled with Scripture but conducted in a prayerless vacuum becomes a heady, rationalized, often legalistic effort. It leaves God out of the equation.
- Heart-based coaching coupled with prayer but lacking Scripture produces an overly emotionalized

faith that misses the objective anchor of God's Word.

- When coaches employ Scripture and prayer alone, without the applied skills of coaching, the truth may never take root and provoke deep-level insights that lead to fruitful action.

Our unique approach to coaching is deeply informed by the seven realities Henry Blackaby taught in his classic work, *Experiencing God.*[2] In that material, Blackaby outlines a sevenfold process through which people experience God:

1. God is always at work around you.
2. God pursues a continuing love relationship with you that is real and personal.
3. God invites you to become involved with Him and His work.
4. God speaks by the Holy Spirit through the Bible, prayer, circumstances, and the church to reveal Himself, His purposes, and His ways.
5. God's invitation for you to work with Him always leads you to a crisis of belief that requires faith and action.
6. You must make major adjustments in your life to join God in what He is doing.
7. You come to know God by experience as you obey Him, and He accomplishes His purposes through you.

---

[2]Henry and Richard Blackaby, and Claude King, *Experiencing God: Knowing and Doing the Will of God* (Nashville: Lifeway Christian Resources, 2006).

In Chapter Three, we will provide a more complete description of the Seven Realities as they apply to coaching.

People often ask us how our approach to coaching relates to "Christian coaching." That question is difficult to answer, because "Christian coaching" means different things to different people. Does it refer to a specialized kind of coaching? Is it any type of coaching a Christian provides? Not everything that is labelled "Christian coaching" fits our understanding of a biblically informed, God-centered approach. While we may use "Christian coaching" and "spiritual leadership coaching" interchangeably, we are referring to the unique coaching model we set forth in this book. While "leadership" is in the title, our understanding and approach extends beyond leadership issues.[3]

People also regularly ask us whether "spiritual leadership coaching" and "spiritual direction" are the same thing. Again, the answer depends on how the term is defined. "Spiritual direction" has been practiced across many faith traditions for centuries. These widely differing approaches always involve a spiritually mature individual who is gifted or trained in the art of honing someone else's spiritual life. While spiritual leadership coaching might be considered a subset of spiritual direction, we cannot endorse everything that is labelled "spiritual direction." Further, the word "direction"

---

[3]For a thorough presentation of our view of leadership, see Henry and Richard Blackaby, *Spiritual Leadership: Moving People on to God's Agenda* (Nashville: B and H Publishing Group, 2011).

implies giving spiritual advice or even orders. We prefer to describe our approach and leave the reader to discern how it compares to other methods.

During our training workshops, we often ask participants to identify which of the Seven Realities from *Experiencing God* typically causes people to seek the help of a coach. The "Crisis of Belief" stage is the most common answer. People certainly desire guidance during a crisis of belief. A spiritually sensitive coach can help people move forward in faith and obedience. Any one of the realities outlined in *Experiencing God*, however, might become an entry point for fruitful coaching as people do the following:

1. Seek to identify where God is at work in their life circumstances.
2. Struggle to know, love, and serve God when He seems distant and impersonal.
3. Make sense of God's calling and invitation to join in His work.
4. Seek God's will as they read Scripture, pray, discern God's hand in their circumstances, and respond to insights from fellow Christians.
5. Gather the courage to follow through on the commitments God calls them to make.
6. Make the necessary adjustments to move forward in response to God's prompting.
7. Experience God in deeper ways as they walk with Him daily.

Each of the Seven Realities can become a launching pad for effective coaching conversations. Coaches must listen carefully and pay attention to ways God is working in the person's life. They can then probe with powerful questions and observations that bring God's agenda into focus. In Chapter Nine, we include examples of powerful questions coaches might ask as the client experiences each stage of the Seven Realities.

CONCLUSION

Spiritual leadership coaching is a deep and rich way to help someone know and do God's will. To be effective, the coach must be spiritually attuned. Spiritual leadership coaching consists of helping people connect the dots between God's activity and their life circumstances (Gal. 5:25) and then step forward in faith and obedience.

FOR REFLECTION AND DISCUSSION

1. Before reading this book, what was your view of coaching? How does it align with what we presented in this chapter? How has your understanding changed?

2. How involved do you expect God to be in a coaching experience? Are you comfortable with the focus being on God and not the coach?

3. Which feels more natural to you: demonstrating your expertise, or serving as a facilitator for people as they seek to find answers for themselves?

4. What might you need to "unlearn" before you can become a better coach?

CHAPTER 2

Character Counts

*And not only that, but we also rejoice in our afflictions,
because we know that affliction produces endurance,
endurance produces proven character, and proven
character produces hope.*
Romans 5:3-4

*Some are blessed with physical and mental facility, but
none are more prized than the one who has developed
true character.*
Greg Henry Quinn

A LIFE-CHANGING TEN-MINUTE CONVERSATION

A prominent denominational leader approached me (Richard) after I delivered a message at a pastors' event. "I need to tell you a story about your father," he said. The leader admitted that he had been a rebellious college student. He rejected his parents' faith and pursued pleasure with abandon. One day, a friend invited him to tag along on a ski trip. While he had no desire to attend a Christian retreat, he was intrigued by skiing, as well as by some of the girls who were going. He resigned himself to endure a few sermons.

Henry Blackaby spoke at that conference. His sincerity and passion captivated the college student more than his sermons did. The young man felt compelled to speak to him after the service. He was apprehensive about talking to a pastor, so he strategically positioned himself at the end of the long line of people waiting to meet my father. Lunchtime was approaching, and the college student assumed Henry would soon leave to eat lunch or attend his next meeting. Instead, he patiently spoke to each person in line.

When the college student's turn came, he and my father were the only two people left in the large auditorium. Tears filled the denominational leader's eyes as he recalled that event decades later.

"The next ten minutes changed my life," he said. His conversation with my father impacted him so strongly that he turned his life back to God. He ultimately became a pastor and led several large congregations before he was chosen to oversee an entire convention of churches.

What struck me about the man's story was that my father's sermon had not changed him. In fact, he couldn't remember it. My father's books had not impacted him; he had not written any at that point. The leader could not even recall what my father said. But he distinctly remembered being in the presence of someone who was genuine, passionate, and wise. He had finally found someone whose opinion he wanted to hear.

Most people want to impact others, yet such influence is often elusive. A boy might ignore his mother's pleading to clean his room. Church members may disregard a pastor's church growth strategy. The sheer number or volume of a person's words does not determine their power. Even truthful words may fail to inspire change. The most effective coaches are those whose character is consistent with their message.

THE POWER OF AN AUTHENTIC LIFE

People want to be close to those individuals whose walk with God glistens with authenticity, because, like Moses descending the mountain, their spiritual glow cannot be counterfeited (Ex. 34:29-35). These spiritual role models dwell in God's presence, and His glory transforms them (2 Cor. 3:18).

There are no shortcuts to spiritual transformation. Someone might adopt King James' English and pontificate on technical theological matters, but others will quickly discern whether the person's relationship with Christ is genuine, growing, and dynamic. The world does not need human advice; it needs a word from God. As Henry Blackaby said to powerful effect, "You cannot take people farther spiritually than you have gone yourself." The key to coaches' effectiveness is not their eloquence but their Christ-likeness.

Coaches must walk closely with God, because spiritual leadership coaching is performed on holy ground. They must take off their spiritual sandals. That is, they must reverently recognize and respond to almighty God's activity in their midst before they can effectively guide others.

Does this spiritual truth imply that only super saints should consider becoming coaches? No. But it underscores the reality that God will not be mocked (Gal. 6:7). Since coaches engage in spiritual work, they must be tuned to God's frequency.

How can coaches live in such a manner that God uses them to change people's lives? Here are some guidelines:

- Since God speaks through the *Bible*, coaches must persistently seek the Person and will of God through His Word.

- Because He also speaks through *prayer*, coaches must prioritize their conversations with almighty God. Great coaches are great listeners. This skill applies to their relationship with God. The Lord declares: *"Call to Me and I will answer you and tell you great and incomprehensible things you do not know"* (Jer. 33:3). Unfortunately, modern prayer is often a monologue. People speak and expect God to listen. Perhaps this disconnect is the reason so many people find prayer dissatisfying and ineffective. Simply telling God about a need does not necessarily reveal His answers. For that, people must stop speaking and tune their spiritual senses to His voice. If coaches do not know how to discern God's answers to their own problems, they will be unable to help others seek His solutions.

- God sometimes speaks through life *circumstances.* We call this method, "connecting the spiritual dots." Since God is at work all around people, they must learn to recognize His activity in their ordinary life. For example, a woman might have prayed for financial provision. Suddenly, she hears about a chance to take on some freelance work. The Holy Spirit can help her discern if this opportunity is a random coincidence or an answer to prayer. A man may have sensed he needs to spend more time at home with his children. The next day, he learns about a new position in his company. The job pays less than what he is currently earning, but it offers a better work-life balance. The Holy Spirit can help him determine whether the new job is a God-ordained opportunity. Life is merely a random series of events until people recognize God's activity in their circumstances.

- Finally, God speaks through the *Church.* Spiritual communities provide valuable wisdom, feedback, and accountability to their participants. If coaches do not allow others to speak truth into their life, how can they effectively assist others? Unfortunately, we occasionally meet people whose lives are in terrible disarray, yet they want to counsel others. These people love to proffer advice, but they hate receiving it! Separated, unaccountable Christians are weak Christians. And weak Christians cannot war effectively in battles of the soul.

CONCLUSION

Coaches must manage themselves well if they desire to guide others. Whether anyone currently wants to enlist their coaching services is irrelevant. They should invite God to work in their life today so they are prepared to help others when the time comes.

Henry Blackaby and Claude King penned the paradigm-shattering book *Experiencing God* in 1990. The insights it contains have transformed countless lives around the globe. In the next chapter, we will review each of these realities from a spiritual leadership coaching perspective and examine other core assumptions that inform our approach.

FOR REFLECTION AND DISCUSSION

Take a moment to think about the three people who have had the greatest positive influence on you, both personally and spiritually.

1. What character qualities did these people possess that stood out to you?
2. Think of your interactions with them. What did they say or do for you? What did they *not* do for you?
3. What questions did they ask that most powerfully impacted you?
4. What can their lives teach you that will help you grow as a Christian and coach?

CHAPTER 3

The Underlying Core: Foundational Assumptions

In essentials Unity, In non-essentials Liberty, In all things Charity.
Rupertus Meldenius

Two are better than one because they have a good reward for their efforts. For if either falls, his companion can lift him up, but pity the one who falls without another to lift him up.
Ecclesiastes 4:9-10

People regularly tell me (Richard) about life-changing experiences they have had. These stories often involve the book *Experiencing God*. One young lady said she grew up with an abusive father and entered adulthood with deep pain, resentment, and distrust. She assumed she was worthless. She believed fathers were hurtful, condemning people. She also deeply distrusted men. Not surprisingly, this woman experienced much heartache and disappointment.

When she took the course *Experiencing God*, she became extremely angry that the study portrayed God as a loving father. She did not understand how people in her study group could speak so affectionately about God when she was certain He would eventually disappoint or harm them.

Then she experienced a spiritual breakthrough. As she completed her daily homework for the course, the Holy Spirit opened her eyes to God's true nature. She realized she had been judging her heavenly Father by her experience with a sinful earthly father. She should have instead compared her earthly father to her perfect, loving heavenly Father.

This revelation transformed the woman's life. She realized she had a father who loved her, and she was finally free to live the abundant life God always intended for her to enjoy.

THE SEVEN REALITIES

Some people view God as a distant deity. Others think of Him as vengeful and condemning. Our view of God is best outlined in the Seven Realities of *Experiencing God*. Here is a brief description of each spiritual reality:

1. God is always at work around you.

"My Father is still working, and I am working also" (John 5:17).

Some Christians live as though God is an absentee landlord. They believe He gave the Ten Commandments, then retreated into the background. One executive client I (Bob) coached operated under this worldview. Though a practicing Christian, he used his God-given talents to achieve his own goals. He experienced some success, but he often grew frustrated and disillusioned when his well-constructed plans failed. He eventually realized he could exert a much greater impact if his life were fully aligned with God's agenda and power.

Spirit-sensitive coaches know that God is always at work. They assume God is present in their client's life, so they watch for His activity. They direct their client's attention to His work by listening deeply and posing powerful questions. People are often disoriented to God and His purposes, so they do not recognize His hand in their life, even when it is obvious to others.

2. God pursues a continuing love relationship with you that is real and personal.

"The LORD appeared to him far away. I have loved you with an everlasting love; therefore, I have continued to extend faithful love to you" (Jer. 31:3).

Coaches must seek to understand their client's attitude toward God's gracious, relentless love. Some people cannot see beyond a loss they experienced or a heavy, unfair burden they carry. Others project deep frustrations onto God, blocking the truth from sight. Coaches might consider the following questions when gauging the person's posture before God:

- In what ways is he pursuing, ignoring, and/or running from God's love?
- Does she find delight in Him or merely obey Him out of duty and fear?
- Would he describe God in terms of a doctrine to believe or a person to love?

Sometimes people sense what God wants to do in their life, but they are afraid to relinquish control. Coaches can help them learn to entrust their life into God's powerful, capable hands.

3. God invites you to become involved with Him in His work.

"If anyone serves Me, he must follow Me. Where I am, there My servant also will be. If anyone serves Me, the Father will honor him" (John 12:26).

The underlying goal of spiritual leadership coaching is not to enable people to become happy, well-adjusted, or successful in their career. Rather, coaches help people identify God's plan for their life and take confident steps toward fulfilling that calling. Coaches undertake this role humbly, knowing their clients are ultimately responsible for discerning and responding to God's initiative. Coaches serve as spiritual midwives, guiding people toward God's purpose for their lives.

4. God speaks by the Holy Spirit through the Bible, prayer, circumstances and the church to reveal Himself, His purposes, and His ways.

"The words that I have spoken to you are spirit and are life" (John 6:63).

Coaches must always be keenly aware that their words cannot set people free. Only God's truth can do that (John 8:32). When God is clearly speaking to someone, coaches should be wary of cluttering the conversation with unnecessary words. Rather, they should listen prayerfully and ask relevant questions that highlight God's voice as He speaks through Scripture, prayer, circumstances, and other believers.

The problem many people experience is not that God is silent, but that they do not recognize His voice. They may expect Him to speak audibly or through an ecstatic experience. Yet God may be all but shouting at them through their spouse's voice!

We worked with one businessman who accepted a job that was entirely wrong for him. He explained that he had prayed for God's guidance, but heaven remained silent. So he acted based on his best human reasoning. The result was disastrous. As we probed further, he confessed that his wife had opposed the job change from the beginning. His prayer group had also expressed grave concerns. Even his teenage son had made a cautionary comment. Yet he proceeded anyway, claiming God had not spoken. In fact, he *had* heard from God repeatedly.

He just hadn't recognized that his friends and family were the bearers of God's message.

Coaches help people discern God's voice. Though His character remains consistent, His mode of communication can vary widely. He might have spoken through a sermon at church previously, but now He speaks daily through the client's quiet times. God does not want people to trust in a formula, but in a relationship. Frederick Buechner stresses the necessity of slowing down and focusing on that relationship by paying attention to what God says and does:

> Listen for God, stop and watch and wait for him. To love God means to pay attention and be mindful, be open to the possibility that God is with you in ways that, unless you have your eyes open, you may never glimpse. He speaks words that, unless you have your ears open, you may never hear.[1]

Supposed followers of Jesus too often fail to follow Him because they are busy chasing petty urgencies and trivialities! People's own sinful desires pull them away to lesser pursuits that have no eternal significance.

One of the best ways to help people hear from God is to follow faith pioneer George Mueller's example and guide people to pray until their heart no longer has its own will in the matter.[2] People are best able to hear from God when they are willing to obey whatever He says.

---

[1] Frederick Buechner, *The Remarkable Ordinary* (Grand Rapids, Michigan: Zondervan, 2017), 36-37.

[2] George Mueller and A.E.C. Brooks, *Answers to Prayer* (Scotts Valley, California: Create Space, 2017), 7.

5. God's invitation for you to work with Him always leads you to a crisis of belief that requires faith and action.

"He replied, 'What is impossible with man is possible with God'" (Luke 18:27).

Most people view a crisis as something negative they should avoid at all costs. But God's work is always God-sized. Without faith, it is *impossible* to please God (Heb. 11:6). As Henry Blackaby often warned, people want to walk by sight but call it faith! God will regularly introduce challenges into people's lives that require them to trust Him.

People often seek a Christian coach's services when they are facing a God-sized undertaking. Coaches aid clients as they follow God into the terrifying unknown. This task is precarious. Spiritual leadership coaches must be spiritually attuned and courageous enough to ask hard questions. Being too severe in the coaching process can send the client into a reactive shell. Approaching faith challenges carelessly might leave clients more baffled than focused. And when coaches—avoiding confrontation or pain—fail to ask hard questions, clients might settle into spiritual mediocrity.

While crises of belief can be uncomfortable or frightening, they are also exhilarating. Most people do not merely want to exist; they want to live! These faith-stretching personal growth moments often lead to people's greatest successes and produce their most cherished memories. This reality is what makes spiritual leadership coaching so rewarding.

6. You must make major adjustments in your life to join God in what He is doing.

"So Moses took his wife and sons, put them on a donkey, and returned to the land of Egypt. And Moses took God's staff in his hand" (Ex. 4:20).

When God speaks, He transforms people. After God spoke, Noah began constructing an ark, Abram left his country, Moses returned to Egypt, Mary prepared to face a scandal, and Peter and Andrew left their fishing business. People cannot remain where they are and go with God!

A woman approached me (Richard) at a conference once and said God told her to begin a woman's ministry at her church. Much to her disappointment, however, her husband was unsupportive. He did not think she had the necessary leadership skills to develop such a ministry. She asked me if I thought her husband would eventually support her if she stepped out in faith. I told her he might not.

"But are you saying that if I start this ministry, the women in my church will support my efforts?" she asked.

"No, I'm not," I replied. "But that doesn't matter. What matters is that you respond immediately to what God is telling you."

This woman knew what God wanted her to do, but she was unwilling to move forward until she was assured of success.

Spiritual leadership coaches help people align their life with God's initiative. Clients may know what God wants them to do, but need help determining what steps to take first. Coaches also help people identity and establish systems of accountability so they can experience success.

7. You come to know God by experience as you obey Him and He accomplishes His work through you.

"When Jacob awoke from his sleep, he said, 'Surely the LORD is in this place, and I did not know it'" (GEN. 28:16).

"Then their eyes were opened, and they recognized him, but he disappeared from their sight. They said to each other, 'Weren't our hearts burning within us while he was talking with us on the road and explaining the Scriptures to us'" (Luke 24:31-32)?

In the gold rush days, prospectors carried their bags of gilded discoveries to an assayer who weighed the gold and determined its degree of purity. Spiritual leadership coaches are spiritual assayers who use questions and prayer to help other people understand and evaluate their circumstances, particularly after an encounter with God. Coaches help them understand the content of what God said, as well as the magnitude of what He asked. These conversations can lead to dramatic spiritual breakthroughs that become life markers in clients' ever-deepening walk with God.

Many people grow up hearing sermons about God's activity in the Bible and throughout history. It is supremely satisfying for coaches when their clients realize that they, too, can experience God as He accomplishes His will through their life.

OTHER CORE BELIEFS THAT INFORM OUR APPROACH

Relationship-Based Coaching

In the medical field, people often speak of a doctor's bedside manner. Some physicians have a good one. Others do not. A doctor's primary responsibility, though, is diagnosing illnesses accurately and prescribing the most effective treatment plan. A pleasant demeanor is a bonus.

Spiritual leadership coaches help clients encounter a Savior whose two greatest commandments are relational: to love God and to love one's neighbor (Mark 12:28-31). People skills are, therefore, crucial for effective leadership coaching. Coaches must be able to sense their client's emotions and struggles. Building a relationship of trust with the person being coached is essential. Coaches will have great difficulty helping people if they do not practice empathy and sensitivity. Highly effective coaches have a variety of relational tools at their disposal. As they sense their client's emotional state, they can take the approach that is best suited to the situation.

Christ-like Character

Coaches gain credibility when they demonstrate a Christ-like character in their own life. As coaches display the fruit of the Spirit (Gal. 5:22-23), their clients experience God's love, joy, peace, patience, kindness, and goodness as well. If, on the other hand, coaches exhibit pride or impatience or defensiveness during their coaching interactions, they have clearly failed. If they cannot control themselves, they will be unable to lead or inspire confidence in others.

A Come Alongside Relationship

Inequality characterizes most learning relationships: parent to child, teacher to pupil, mentor to novice. Undoubtedly, a spiritual leadership coach possesses expertise the coachee lacks. Effective spiritual leadership coaches, however, refrain from indulging themselves in teaching, preaching, or directing. They do not lead clients toward a predetermined, coach-driven goal. Rather, they participate in a peer-to-peer relationship with their clients. They come alongside them and help them discover, embrace, and live out God's purposes. This approach can be surprising for the coachee who might expect to receive specific answers or advice.

Coaches Get Out of the Way

Only two voices matter in a coaching conversation: God's and the coachee's. Coaches should support rather than impede that divine conversation. Their contributions should merely keep the interaction between the two primary parties moving toward God's agenda. A good rule of thumb is for coaches to speak no more than 20% of the time in a coaching conversation. They should support their interjections with good questions and a listening posture.

CONCLUSION

Spiritual leadership coaching rests on certain convictions. Coaches who use the approach outlined in this book view God's work in people's lives through the theological lens of the Seven Realities of *Experiencing God*. They practice relationship-based coaching while demonstrating Christ-like character and keeping the focus on God's activity. These practices spring from the conviction that God has revealed Himself in human history and continues to speak to people through His Word, prayer, circumstances, and fellow believers. In the next chapter, we will turn our attention to the Bible and coaching.

FOR REFLECTION AND DISCUSSION

1. Which of the Seven Realities do you find most difficult to practice? Why?
2. How empathetic are you when relating to others? What habits might you practice to grow in empathy?
3. What do people need more from you: answers or understanding?
4. As you read this chapter, what most convicted you? How will you respond?

CHAPTER 4

The Bible and Coaching

Counsel in a person's heart is deep water;
but a person of understanding draws it out.
Proverbs 20:5

For the word of God is living and effective and sharper
than any double-edged sword, penetrating as far as the
separation of soul and spirit, joints and marrow. It is
able to judge the thoughts and intentions of the heart.
Hebrews 4:12

We chuckle at the story of the child who became exasperated by her mother's rules and exclaimed: *"I am able to do all things through Him who strengthens me!"* (Phil. 4:13). While her Scripture memorization is commendable, her theological application is questionable!

Like the willful child, many people misuse Scripture in order to justify their actions. Even Satan quoted Scripture when he tempted Jesus (Luke 4:9-11). For that reason, coaches must use the Bible carefully and reverently. When mishandled, it can become a club to condemn others or a license to sin. The apostle Paul urged young Timothy to *"be diligent to present yourself to God as one approved, a worker who doesn't need to be ashamed, correctly teaching the word of truth"* (2 Tim. 2:15). With practice and study, coaches can learn to employ Scripture skillfully.

The word "coach" was first used, according to the *Online Etymology Dictionary,* to describe a type of horse-drawn carriage that originated in Hungary. Simply put, a coach was a means of transporting passengers and goods from one place to another. Likewise, spiritual leadership coaches help people move from where they are to where God wants them to be.

Though the word "coach" is not found in the Bible, Scripture clearly emphasizes people's need for godly counsel. One of the earliest examples of such guidance is found in Exodus 18. Moses' father-in-law, Jethro, helped Moses understand that he needed to delegate leadership. The load Moses carried as his nation's top leader overwhelmed him. From Moses' perspective, the situation was unmanageable and hopeless. But one conversation set him free and led to widespread blessing.

Proverbs contains numerous references to wisdom. Proverbs 25:11 states, *"A word spoken at the right time is like gold apples in silver settings."* In Proverbs 17:27, a calm and listening presence—a quality of effective coaching—is extoled: *"The one who has knowledge restrains his words, and one who keeps a cool head is a person of understanding."* Ecclesiastes 9:17-18 asserts,

"The calm words of the wise are heeded more than the shouts of a ruler over fools. Wisdom is better than weapons of war, but one sinner can destroy much good." Wisdom Literature clearly acknowledges the power of a well-placed word!

The book of Job also highlights the value of wisdom. Job declared, *"Wisdom and strength belong to God; counsel and understanding are His"* (Job 12:13). On its own, this verse exposes the true source of wisdom and understanding. But when it is placed in context, its coaching implications expand considerably.

In the previous chapter, Job's so-called friend Zophar assumed Job's suffering was a result of unconfessed sin. He, like Job, acknowledged God as the source of wisdom. But rather than seeking God with Job, he hastily embraced a simplistic conclusion. Job responded sarcastically: *"No doubt you are the people, and wisdom will die with you. But I also have a mind like you; I am not inferior to you. Who doesn't know the things you are talking about"* (Job 12:2-3)? Job never doubted God's wisdom. But he desperately needed friends to help him discover God's answers.

I (Bob) lead a small group of middle-aged professional couples in a weekly Bible study. I prepare for our meetings diligently, because I know the attendees are sharp people who have also studied the passage. I prayerfully pour over each verse, consult excellent commentaries, and develop my key insights. I am no longer surprised, however, when God grants group members insights that are deeper than mine. Why? Because I remember Jesus' words about the ministry of the Holy Spirit in John 14:26. Coaches must learn to trust His lead as they ask insightful Spirit-led questions.

Christian coaches are most effective when they understand that their primary task is not to explain or interpret other people's painful circumstances but to connect them to God. Job's friends, with their easy clichés and quick judgments, failed that test. They behaved like high-priced consultants who arrive with pre-set answers in their brief case. They assumed they already knew the answers to Job's questions, so they did not journey with him.

LEADERSHIP COACHING

Spiritual leadership coaching is an important, often underutilized means of providing wise guidance. It serves a vital role in the Christian community, alongside teaching, preaching, spiritual mentoring, and discipleship. It is most effective when undergirded by the following spiritual gifts: *exhortation* (Rom. 12:8), *wisdom* (1 Cor. 12:8), and *discernment* (1 Cor. 12:10).

EXHORTATION: to use words of encouragement, comfort, and consolation to help others fulfil their God-given purpose (Greek word: *paraklesis*, which means calling to one's side).

WISDOM: applying knowledge and spiritual truths in practical ways to decision-making and daily life situations.

DISCERNMENT: the ability to determine whether a behavior or teaching is from God, Satan, or human reasoning.[1]

USING SCRIPTURE IN SPIRITUAL LEADERSHIP COACHING

Coaches approach Scripture differently than other church leaders do. Preachers proclaim the Bible through sermons. Teachers lead Bible studies. Mature Christians might employ Scripture in one-on-one mentoring sessions. Each of these methods can be effective. But the Word of God may also speak directly to an individual's heart. Hebrews 4:12 declares: *"For the word of God is living and effective and sharper than any double-edged sword, penetrating as far as the separation of soul and spirit, joints and marrow. It is able to judge the thoughts and intentions of the heart."* This high-powered quality of Scripture makes it an essential tool in a coaching encounter.

If God speaks to people directly through the Bible, what role does a spiritual leadership coach play, and how does it differ from preaching or teaching biblical principles?

First, coaches do not assume they possess all Bible knowledge. Coaches should not merely recite a Bible verse every time a client mentions a problem! People often know what the Bible says, but they struggle to apply its truths to their life. A coach's job is to draw out

---

[1] *Ministry Tools Resource Center,* http://mintools.com/gifts-list.htm (Accessed August 23, 2014).

the biblical principles God has already planted in the person's heart and to help their clients *"humbly receive the implanted word, which is able to save your souls"* (James 1:21). The following questions may help reveal that divinely planted word:

- When you think about your situation, which Bible verses, stories, or principles come to mind?
- What do you consider the essential message of that Scripture passage?
- With which character in this story do you most identify? How so?
- Which part of this passage most frightens or troubles you? What does your response reveal about your values?
- How do you think this passage applies to your situation?
- What might God be saying to you?
- What would obedience to this truth look like for you? What is the first step you should take?
- What commitment are you ready to make to align yourself with God's Word?

A well-chosen question can bring a Scripture passage powerfully to bear on the person being coached.

My (Richard) father, Henry Blackaby, once encountered a veteran who was deeply traumatized by his time in Vietnam. In order to survive his deployment, he steeled himself to the horrors he experienced until his emotions were deadened. He returned to his family and friends after his tour of duty, but he had become hardened and detached. His inability to express emotion strained his marriage and hurt his children. His love and compassion had seemingly died on the battlefield.

As Henry spoke with the man, he sensed God leading him to cite Ezekiel 36:26: *"I will give you a new heart and put a new spirit within you; I will remove your heart of stone and give you a heart of flesh."* Henry asked the veteran if he would like God to turn his heart of stone into a heart of flesh. As he pondered Henry's question, the Holy Spirit convinced the man that he could indeed experience the radical life transformation he read about in the Bible. He prayed with Henry.

"It's gone! It's gone! My heart of stone is gone!" he exclaimed a moment later. Tears of joy streamed down his face. The work of the Holy Spirit through Scripture had dramatically changed his life.

Second, the Bible is an instrument of grace and insight, not coercion. Inexperienced coaches occasionally use Scripture to pressure or manipulate people. At times, taking a direct or pointed approach may be necessary. But even when dealing with immature believers, a good question rather than a pre-set answer can spark a holy hunger that leads to deeper understanding. Coaches ought to avoid using Scripture as a trump card that squelches discussion. The Bible is the ultimate authority for the Christian life, but the coachee might need to grapple with its meaning and application. Simply spouting off a Bible verse is not enough. The coach must help people understand and embrace the verse's message in their own circumstances.

Third, the Bible is not an instruction manual for every situation. Jesus said, *"You will know the truth, and the truth will set you free"* (John 8:32). God's truth is embedded in the Bible, but Scripture does not directly address every issue or situation. It does not tell people which job to take or whether to accept a promotion. It does not direct bosses to fire an underperforming employee or extend one more chance. Certain passages speak to those issues, but such decisions are often nuanced with compelling arguments on multiple sides. What if the Bible doesn't give a clear answer? Through prayer, the Holy Spirit can guide people to apply Scriptures to specific situations.

When people submit to the authority of God's Word, they acknowledge the Bible's prerogative over people's opinions. Wise coaches encourage people to measure the counsel they receive—even from their coach—against Scripture. Even coaches are wrong sometimes!

Coaches may occasionally need to intervene when people misapply a verse or passage. But they should use corrections sparingly so people learn to interpret Scripture for themselves. One way I (Bob) handle this situation is to signal that I am changing "hats." I might say, "Do you mind if I take off my coach hat for a moment, and share my understanding of this passage?" I will then impart a biblical truth I feel is important for the person to consider. However, except for clear and important departures from truth that require correction, the focus should remain squarely on what God is saying to the client, not on the coach's insights. A coach approach requires the leader to trust that God's Word works powerfully, even when people are not Bible scholars. Ultimately, the Holy Spirit is the person's spiritual teacher.

CONCLUSION

A well-made automobile contains a myriad of highly interdependent parts that work in harmony to achieve an exceptional ride. Likewise, spiritual guidance requires spiritual maturity, awareness of God's Word, prayer, and effective coaching skills. We turn next to prayer and God's agenda.

FOR REFLECTION AND DISCUSSION:

1. How has God provoked you to new ways of thinking? Give examples.
2. When can a direct use of Scripture be helpful? When would a coach approach be more effective?
3. When have you seen someone employ the Bible in a harsh or manipulative way? How did that affect your faith?
4. How well do you know Scripture? Can you handle it easily and accurately enough to guide others with it? How might you become more proficient in your biblical understanding?

CHAPTER 5

Prayer and God's Agenda

If we truly love people, we will desire for them far more than it is within our power to give them, and this leads us to prayer.
Richard Foster

Prayer, I have discovered, is less about what I say and more about what I hear.
Susan Cosio

I (Richard) had just finished speaking at a gathering of international evangelists when Jim (name has been changed) approached me and told me his story. He had experienced the worst crisis of his life twenty years earlier when his wife committed adultery and divorced him. His denomination forbade divorcees from serving in his ministry position, so he resigned. His final work-related responsibility was to attend a conference where my father, Henry, was the keynote speaker.

As Jim was walking through the lobby after one of the services, he felt someone punch his arm. He looked up and was surprised to see my father standing beside him. Someone had told Henry about the anguish Jim was experiencing, and my father wanted to meet with him. Henry's schedule, however, was booked solid until ten o'clock that night. Henry asked if Jim would be willing to meet him in the prayer garden shortly after ten o'clock. Startled by Henry's invitation, Jim agreed.

During their meeting in the prayer garden, Henry listened to Jim's story. Afterward, he did not evaluate Jim's situation or offer advice. In that painful, confusing moment, he began to pray. Henry pleaded with God to reveal His infinite love to the hurting man. He asked God to heal his brokenness and grant him peace and hope. Henry cited a Scripture verse that promised the man's latter days would be more prosperous than his former days (Job 8:7). Many people had prayed for Jim, but he had never heard someone cry out to God on his behalf. My father sought God so earnestly Jim was certain God would respond. Throughout the next few days, two other people shared the same verse with him.

After the conference, Jim left his job and relocated to another state. A large Christian organization eventually invited him to serve in their international ministry. He met and married a godly woman who became his faithful, loving companion. He said that whenever people ask how he managed to have such a blessed, productive, joyful life, he tells them it began with Henry Blackaby's prayer!

People sometimes face excruciating circumstances. Their problems may not have obvious solutions. Coaches do them no favors by offering their opinion or best guess. Human advice cannot change a life, but one encounter with God can. Coaches must never underestimate the enormous life-changing power that is available through prayer.

Buried deep within the human heart is an unquenchable longing. Ecclesiastes' author declared that God has placed eternity in the human heart, yet people do not fully understand it (Ecc. 3:11). God's purpose and plan for people is far greater than they could imagine (Eph. 1:10; 3:20). Leading someone to understand God's agenda requires more than skillfully employed coaching techniques. Coaches must reach beyond their human wisdom to the secret places of God's heart through intercessory prayer.

Making assumptions comes naturally. People might notice a discouraged man and think, "He just needs to get over it!" Or perhaps they encounter a woman who is struggling financially and immediately determine what changes she should make. But they don't necessarily know the hurting people as well as they suppose. They haven't experienced the depth of their disappointments and fears. They are unaware of the life events that shaped their perspective. They do not fully comprehend what God intends for them. Godly coaches understand that engaging in intercessory prayer is like stepping into a tornado. The destination is uncertain, but the ride is thrilling.

Coaches should not feel awkward about praying with their clients. Not only does prayer set the stage for God to speak, but it also communicates clearly to clients that their coach is seeking God's best for them. Here are some principles coaches should consider regarding prayer:

1. *Coaches should pray for clients before they meet with them.* Coaches can prepare for a coaching session in many ways, but the most important is through prayer. Coaches do not always know the best approach to take with a client. They may be oblivious to the baggage their client brings to the table. A person may arrive at the meeting distracted, angry, or fearful because of an experience earlier that day. When coaches pray for their clients, God prepares both the clients and the coaches.

We know a coach who prayed fervently for a client to find freedom from some issues that were oppressing him. As the coach prayed, God suddenly revealed the man's situation to him. During their next session, the coach probed with several questions related to the Lord's recent revelation. Issues began bubbling to the surface, and the client was soon sobbing. The coach told us he was absolutely certain he would not have pursued that line of questioning had God not opened his understanding through prayer.

2. *Spiritual Coaching is primarily about God and His purposes, not the client's desires.* Proverbs 19:21 states, *"Many plans are in a person's heart, but the LORD's decree*

will prevail. "Secular coaches discover what people want and help them achieve it. Spiritual leadership coaches probe beyond their client's wishes to seek God's agenda.

While I (Bob) was a campus minister, an international student joined an *Experiencing God* group I led. He only participated in our ministry for a single semester before returning to his predominantly Muslim home nation. Decades later, he messaged me on social media and told me his story. As so often happens, he returned to his home country with his American degree and sought to accumulate wealth. But God thwarted his plans, reminding him of a commitment he made during the *Experiencing God* study. The young man fully embraced God's agenda and has since implemented a church planting movement in a region that is officially closed to the Gospel. He desired to parlay a coveted degree to financial success. But God planned to transform a nation!

People who enlist a spiritual leadership coach often wish to connect more deeply and authentically with God. Coaches do them a disservice when they focus solely on the clients' goals rather than on God's activity in their life. As coaches humbly seek God's guidance, they communicate that they do not have all the answers, but they know the One who does!

3. Spiritual truth is revealed, not discovered. In John 7, the crowd tried to understand the source of Jesus' profound wisdom using human reasoning. But Jesus cut to the quick when He declared, *". . . My teaching isn't mine but is from the One who sent Me. If anyone wants to do His will, he will know whether the teaching is from God or whether I am speaking on My own"* (John 7:16-17). Jesus taught that people cannot discover divine truth; God reveals it to those who surrender their heart to His will.

Of course, surrendering one's heart is easier said than done. People might say they want God's will to be done, but the human heart is insidiously deceptive (Jer. 17:9). A person may assume he trusts God, but fear of failure might motivate his actions. Or someone may believe she desires God's guidance, but an earthly father who suffered chronic unemployment might have taught her to obsess over finances. Only God can change a heart. Coaches can, however, facilitate God's transformational activity through prayer.

4. Spiritual leadership coaches lead people to experience God for themselves. Spiritual leadership coaches do not enter God's presence to retrieve treasures for others. Rather, they open doors for others to enter God's presence. Then they help their clients understand and apply God's self-revelation in tangible ways.

Questions are often the most useful coaching tool, especially when people's hearts have been prepared through prayer. Coaches may first ask clients to pray silently as God reveals His will and activity to them. After praying, coaches should assume God spoke (Matt. 7:7). Here are some follow-up questions coaches can ask after a season of silent prayer:

1. What divine thoughts or impressions did you experience while praying?
2. When was the last time God gave you an assignment you resisted?
3. Where is God in this situation? What do you think He is doing or saying to you right now?
4. If you were in my shoes, what advice would you give me (Note: this question may seem human-centered, but it can effectively draw out commitments God is calling a person to make)?
5. What does obedience look like in this situation?
6. What will obedience cost you? What will disobedience cost you?
7. What commitment(s) are you ready to make right now?
8. Considering your options, which choice most reflects the peace of Christ within you (Col. 3:15-16)?

Finally, we encourage coaches to pray in faith for their clients, remaining confident that God will answer. They should avoid praying in an insincere, monotonous, cliché-riddled manner. Instead, they ought to talk to God as if He were sitting in the third chair in the room. Coaches should ask God to reveal His heart and will. Clients may feel that their heart was somehow stirred while the coach prayed. They might even need to wipe tears from their eyes. They may sincerely thank their coach for interceding on their behalf. When coaches join God's activity, they are swept up into the breathtaking work of the Creator of the universe. No other experience can compare!

CONCLUSION

God is always at work in and around people. Coaches should not substitute their agenda for God's. They ought to make the same commitment for their clients as Samuel pledged to the ancient Israelites, *"As for me, I vow that I will not sin against the LORD by ceasing to pray for you. I will teach you the good and right way"* (1 SAM. 12:23). Their prayers should emulate Paul's prayer for the believers in Ephesus:

> *"I never stop giving thanks for you as I remember you in my prayers. I pray that the God of our LORD Jesus Christ, the glorious Father, would give you the Spirit of wisdom and revelation in the knowledge of him. I pray that the eyes of your heart may be enlightened so that you may know what is the hope of his calling, what is the wealth of his glorious inheritance in the saints, and what is the immeasurable greatness of his power toward us who believe . . ."* (Eph. 1:16-19).

Oswald Chambers said, *"Prayer does not fit us for the greater work; prayer is the greater work."* Coaches must not fail to pray for those they serve. And when they pray, they should pay close attention to God's response. When coupled with prayer, effective coaching skills help turn truth into action. In the following chapters, we will look at twelve skills that can empower coaches to do just that.

FOR REFLECTION AND DISCUSSION

1. How comfortable are you with being still and focusing on what God is saying or doing in your midst (listening prayer)? How comfortable are you with praying with someone you are coaching?

2. Describe a time when your agenda was clearly at odds with God's agenda for you or for someone else. What happened as a result?

3. When was a time you knew you were positively impacted by prayers on your behalf?

4. What question might you ask someone who is struggling to find or follow God's will?

5. How comfortable are you with finding God's answers in prayer?

Relationship-Building Skills

Twelve Essential Coaching Skills

META-SKILLS

- **Relationship-Building**
- Awareness-Raising
- Focusing and Commitment
- Futuring

RELATIONSHIP-BUILDING META-SKILLS

Building a relationship with the person that includes mutual trust, spiritual presence, and active multi-level listening.

RELATIONSHIP-BUILDING SKILLS INCLUDE:

1. Establishing Trust (Chapter 6)
2. Being Spiritually Present (Chapter 7)
3. Active Multi-Level Listening (Chapter 8)
   - Listening to Self
   - Listening to Words
   - Listening Between the Lines
   - Spiritual Listening

Establishing Trust

Love all, trust a few.
William Shakespeare

When people see commitments are met with
consistency, they tend to develop trust. Trust is the key
to persuasion.
Khalid Imran

I (Richard) was recently sitting at the desk in my home office when water began pouring through the ceiling tiles from the floor above. Someone had turned on the jets in the upstairs bathtub, and a major leak ensued. Being new to the area, I didn't know who to call for a repair. I went online and hired a local plumber.

The day of my appointment, a sharply dressed service technician arrived. He was well spoken. He carried a slick tool case. After looking at the motor, he pulled out a high-tech camera and took a picture. He said he would have to order a part and return to install it. He charged $65 for the service call, but he assured me the payment would be applied to the final repair bill. I was relieved to know my bathtub would soon be restored to working order.

When I had not heard from the repair company a week later, I called their office for an update. The man who answered the phone apologized and said they had inadvertently neglected to order the part but would do so immediately. When I called again, I was redirected to the company's voicemail. When I called the next time, the voicemail was full and could not receive any new messages. Apparently, I had enlisted a company that took pictures of problems but did not fix them!

I eventually contacted a second plumber. Now I was skeptical! He was dressed quite sloppily and spoke in a slow drawl. I showed him the defective part the first man had identified and asked how long it would take *him* to order a replacement. After examining it, he said there was nothing wrong with that part. It simply needed a gasket and to be bolted into place properly. He finished quickly and I have never experienced another problem with my bathtub.

The first repairman looked professional. He used advanced technology and technical terminology. But he was a charlatan. The second man gave a sorry first impression, but he soon earned my trust and admiration. I kept the second man's business card and would hire him again in a heartbeat.

Who is trustworthy? Few questions are more pressing as people cautiously navigate the minefields of human relationships. Children naturally trust adults. Sadly, adults often disappoint them. Everyone seems to experience betrayal. Mechanics take advantage of people with little knowledge about cars. Too-good-to-be-true opportunities turn out to be scams. Over time, people tend to become increasingly suspicious. They dread being burned again. Healthy people learn discernment. Some people, however, struggle to trust anyone.

Integrity is especially important for leadership coaches because they often deal with vulnerable people. A painful breach of trust occurs when people share their deepest spiritual longings, fears, or insecurities with a spiritual mentor who ultimately hurts them. Divulging confidential information without permission is one form of betrayal. Trust-erosion can also occur when spiritual guides spout ill-fitting solutions to a person's dilemma because they are too dull or lazy to recognize God's activity.

Trust-building is the ability to establish and maintain confidence and rapport with another person. For some people, building trust comes easily. For others, trust is hard-won.

When I (Bob) was a young college minister, I was invited to preach at a local nursing home. I had been assured that someone would lead music before I spoke. But I discovered two problems upon my arrival. First, the worship leader was a no-show. Second, the venue where I was scheduled to lead the service was a crowded corridor along which the staff had parked half a dozen old souls in wheelchairs. No chapel, no pulpit, no music leader—just me towering over a row of senior citizens!

Not wanting to disappoint them, I tried to lead them in singing "Amazing Grace," a capella, with my less-than-stellar voice. Midway through the second stanza, the lady sitting directly in front of me thrust her gnarled finger toward me and shouted, "Young man, are you making fun of us?"

"No ma'am, I'm just doing the best I can," I replied. Embarrassed, I stumbled through the rest of the song. Then I shared a heartfelt word from Scripture.

When I finished, my detractor piped up once again. "At first, I thought you were just making fun of us old people," she said. "But now I see that you are a sincere, godly young man!"

After my disastrous solo, she saw something trustworthy in my preaching.

One way coaches can build trust with their clients is by establishing "ground rules" for the relationship. These rules clarify what the coach will and will not do for clients, as well as the limits of confidentiality. For example, we assure clients that we will not divulge the details of our conversations to others. But we also warn them that if we believe they are a danger to themselves or others, we may need to inform appropriate authorities. Finally, we tell them what they can expect of us and what we expect from them. Addressing these issues up front allows trust to blossom. Not everyone who reads this book will become a professional coach, but the principles are the same for most relationships.

These are the four Cs necessary for building trust in a coaching relationship:

- Christ-like character
- Competence in what you do
- Commitment to the coachee
- Care for the person that is genuine

As a young minister, someone told me (Bob), "If people know you love them, they will follow you anywhere!" Likewise, when people encounter a coach who has a deep faith, is skilled and committed to their well-being, and truly cares about them, they will open their hearts to that person.

King David led his people with skillful hands and integrity of heart (Psalm 78:72). He was one of the finest leaders in the Bible. He was invincible in battle. He inspired mighty men to serve him loyally and enthusiastically. Scripture identifies the twofold secret to his success. First, he had *skillful hands*. He was good at what he did. People could trust him because they knew he had an astounding track record of success. Second, he had *integrity*. His heart was right with God and others (most of the time!). When people see coaches who manage their own heart and life well, they typically trust them.

We find that trust builds more quickly when clients believe their coach truly cares about them. For example, certain body language—such as leaning in at key moments, maintaining eye contact, and asking for clarification when necessary—can signal that the coach is fully engaged. Conversely, frequently checking text messages, looking at a clock, or yawning conveys that the coach is uninterested in the client's well-being. If the coach is fully prepared for each session, people sense that their coach is dealing with them competently. If coaches are unprepared, late, or forget details the client shared previously, they send the message that they are unprepared to help their client resolve problems. If they listen intently, actively, and perceptively, they convey that they truly want to understand the person's situation. If coaches interrupt or immediately launch into their own thoughts after the client finishes speaking, they signal that they would rather display their own knowledge than listen to their client. When people feel a lack of trust or safety, their brain shuts down their ability to learn. Such behavior can sabotage the coaching process.

Wise coaches also recognize the limits to trust in a coaching relationship. Trust may be tenuous during the first session. The client may only be willing to venture into shallow waters. Over time, however, coaches gain the capacity to lead clients into a deeper place.

One of the first Scripture verses I (Bob) learned as a child was Matthew 7:12, *"Whatever you want others to do for you, do also the same for them."* Coaches should consider what they look for in people they trust. They might even make a checklist of characteristics trustworthy people exhibit, then consider how many of those traits they embody.

CONCLUSION

Trust is a necessary element in the coaching process, and coaches can foster it in numerous ways. But trust is not the only key factor in successful coaching. A spiritual presence is equally important. We'll cover that in the next chapter.

FOR REFLECTION AND DISCUSSION

1. Develop your own "Ten Commandments for Building Trust" list based on characteristics you believe trustworthy people should exhibit.

2. After completing the list, ask yourself, "Which of these qualities do I most need to develop?" You may even ask the same question to others who know you.

3. What first step will you take to improve your trustworthiness?

CHAPTER 7

Being Spiritually Present

If we let ourselves, we shall always be waiting for some distraction or other to end before we can really get down to our work.
C.S. Lewis

And remember, I am with you always. . .
Jesus (Matthew 28:20)

Early in my ministry career, I (Richard) went to a large convention in Orlando with my father, Henry. Around 15,000 people attended an evening event emphasizing international missions. At the close of the service, a missionary hurried over to speak with my father. The man was experiencing turmoil in his work and did not know what to do. Should he challenge his supervisor? Should he ask for a transfer? Should he return to America to be closer to his aging parents? The man desperately needed spiritual guidance.

My father gave the hurting man his undivided attention. Periodically, others noticed my father and shouted greetings to him. At least three people invited him to attend after-meeting receptions for denominational leaders. Yet he focused on the missionary as though he were the only person in the room. The man eventually thanked my father profusely for his time and departed.

Immediately, another man spied my father and eagerly engaged him in conversation. This man was an associate pastor of a large church. His senior pastor was proving to be an ungodly leader. The staff were in disarray. The associate pastor respected the senior pastor's office, but he also knew many church members were suffering because of his ineffectual leadership. What should he do? Again, my father trained his attention on this young pastor and sought the Lord's heart and mind for him.

Each time my father finished one discussion, another person immediately engaged him in earnest conversation. Suddenly, the overhead lights in that cavernous auditorium turned off. I glanced around and discovered that we were the only people left in the room! There had been 15,000 people on the premises, but we outlasted them all! As we hastily departed, I reminded my father of the receptions he had been invited to attend at nearby hotels. By then, however, he simply wanted to return to his hotel room to rest!

When my father interacted with someone, he demonstrated an intense spiritual sensitivity to being "present" with the person. Unsurprisingly, everywhere I go around the world people tell me about a life-changing conversation they had with him.

What is spiritual presence? Let's begin with the term *presence*. The *World English Dictionary* defines presence this way:

— n
1. the state or fact of being present
2. the immediate proximity of a person or thing
3. personal appearance or bearing, esp. of a dignified nature
4. an imposing or dignified personality
5. an invisible spirit felt to be nearby

Consider for a moment individuals who stand out from the crowd. Something about them attracts people's attention. Would their presence best be described as inspiring, motivating, commanding, energized, credible, focused, confident, or compelling? Would another word better describe their persona? While one person may pass unnoticed, others have something extra. Presence comes in many forms:

- *Presence as a speaker or thinker:* an ability to express truths in an engaging, compelling, or motivating fashion.
- *One-on-one presence:* an ability to facilitate life-changing experiences through personal encounters.
- *Leadership presence:* an ability to cast vision, set direction, and propel people to action.

In their book, *Leadership Presence*, Lubar and Halpern define presence as the ability to connect authentically with other people's thoughts and feelings. Once a connection is established, people are more open to that individual's leadership.

According to the International Coach Federation, coaching presence is "the ability to be fully conscious and create spontaneous relationship with the client, employing a style that is open, flexible, and confident." This definition means, in simpler terms, that those with coaching presence pay close attention to their client and adapt their responses positively and confidently to meet the person's needs in the moment. Christian coaches move beyond interpersonal attentiveness to look for ways God is working in the person's life.

Some coaches utilize a technique called "mirroring," matching their words, manner, body posture, and approach to fit the client's unique style. Mirroring tends to put the client at ease. But coaches can use this technique either to serve or manipulate the client, so coaches must closely monitor their motives.

In its most basic sense, being present essentially means to occupy the same space as another person physically. But clients need their coach to be emotionally and spiritually near as well.

Jesus was masterful at being fully present with those He encountered. As He traveled through Jericho one day, the streets teemed with people eager to gain His attention. Suddenly, He stopped. He had spotted a notorious sinner watching from a tree branch. In that culture, climbing a tree would have been humiliating for a grown man. Jesus instantly recognized that His Father was working in Zachaeus' life, for only the wooing of the Holy Spirit could cause the despised tax collector to publicly embarrass himself in such a manner. Jesus urged Zachaeus to come down from the tree quickly, for He intended to eat lunch with him in his home that very hour (Luke 19:1-10). Not only did Jesus recognize His Father's work in a man's life, but He immediately rearranged His schedule so He could join that divine activity.

Everyone has interacted with people who were not truly present. Their body may have been in the vicinity, but their mind was a million miles away! To assist someone effectively, coaches must give the client their full attention. They must ignore distractions and focus intently on the client and God's activity in the person's life. How can they achieve that level of presence?

First, coaches must notice minor details in what clients say and do. When my (Bob) kids first learned to play softball and baseball, their measure of success was quite simple. When batting, they tried to hit the ball. As they progressed as batters, the coach began focusing their attention on smaller areas to hit. He would toss two ping pong balls in the air and tell them to hit the higher or lower ball, training their eyes to notice smaller and smaller details. Eventually, they learned to hit the upper half of the ball to avoid pop-ups. Great players don't just see the ball. They also notice the stitching on the ball and whether the ball is rising, dropping, or curving. Likewise, great spiritual coaches notice nuances. They are keenly sensitive to the words people use, the actions they take, and the reasons they hesitate to take on challenges.

Second, coaches must release their assumptions about people. When discussing his book *Blink* in an interview, Malcolm Gladwell stated, "When you meet someone for the first time, or walk into a house you are thinking of buying, or read the first few sentences of a book, your mind takes about two seconds to jump to a series of conclusions."[1] While Gladwell concedes that first impressions are often right, he notes that they are sometimes wrong. Spiritual coaches must lay aside their preconceived ideas and open their spiritual eyes to the hidden ways God may be working.

Inexperienced coaches are often tempted to reach into their bag of canned solutions without waiting for God to guide them. Spouting answers too quickly, however, can cause great spiritual harm. While the client's problem may sound like an issue the coach has addressed before, skilled coaches understand that no two people are identical. Each person has a distinctive set of hurts, disappointments, victories, critics, and friends. Because God is working to accomplish unique purposes in each individual's life, He may have different plans for two people with similar problems. Finally, the end goal might

---

[1]http://gladwell.com/blink/blink-q-and-a-with-malcolm/ (Accessed August 16, 2017).

not be to solve a problem, but to experience personal growth. If coaches offer solutions too quickly, they may miss the far more important objective of increasing self-awareness and maturity. Effective spiritual coaches remain open and available to the Spirit's guidance. Coaches can only be truly present with someone if they are willing to identify how God is working in the person's life and respond accordingly.

Spiritual presence differs from everyday presence. Spiritual presence reflects and magnifies the immediacy of God's activity and purpose. Spiritual leadership coaches strengthen the connection between people and God through authentic, spiritually sensitive attentiveness to God's work in people's life. In describing the importance of equipping ministry students with this skill, Henri Nouwen stated, "I have concluded that the goal in education and formation for the ministry is continually to recognize the Lord's voice, His face, and His touch in every person we meet."[2] Likewise, Eugene Peterson identified the three essential priorities for pastoral ministry as prayer, Scripture, and spiritual direction:

> **Prayer** is an act in which I bring myself to attention before God.
>
> **Scripture** is an act of attending to God in His speech and action across two millennia in Israel and Christ.

---

[2]Quoted in *Grace Notes: Daily Readings* with Philip Yancey. May 8 reading.

> **Spiritual Direction** is an act of giving attention to what God is doing in the person who happens to be before me in a given moment.[3]

Spiritual presence requires coaches to leave behind their own agendas and attend to God's activity.

Several years ago at a party, I (Richard) began a conversation with a man who was struggling. As we talked, I asked some questions that helped him see his problem differently. He began to identify specific steps he might take to resolve the issue. Everything was going well. Then a well-meaning friend noticed us talking and decided to join our conversation. In an effort to help, the friend interrupted and added his "two cents." He then launched into a long, unrelated story. The hurting man and I both realized the friend was inadvertently derailing what had been an excellent conversation. As tactfully as I could, I attempted to reclaim the conversation and hint that the interloper should stop talking (or find some chips and salsa at the food table and allow us to resume our original discussion!). Unfortunately, a spiritually clueless third party all too often derails redemptive encounters.

Coaches never want to be "that friend" who talks too much and hijacks a potentially life-changing conversation. The most critical exchange occurs between the coachee and God. Coaches are the "third person" in the discussion. Before speaking, they should seek to

---

[3]Eugene H Peterson, *Working the Angles: The Shape of Pastoral Integrity* (Grand Rapids: William B. Eerdmans Publishing Company, 1989), 3.

understand what God is already saying to the individual. They dare not interrupt when God has the floor. Great coaches read the moment and tune in to their client's experience.

To be spiritually present, a person must allow God to move as He wills in a given moment. Relinquishing control might frighten an insecure person, but the Holy Spirit works as He pleases. Jesus was fully present with Nicodemus when He shattered Nicodemus' pre-set notions about the nature of true faith: *"Do not be amazed that I told you that you must be born again. The wind blows where it pleases, and you hear its sound, but you don't know where it comes from or where it is going. So it is with everyone born of the Spirit"* (John 3:7-8). Born-again followers of Jesus should heed Jesus' admonition. A coach's desire for situational control can short-circuit God's movement and prevent spiritual breakthroughs. Coaches must recognize that God was at work in the person's life long before they entered the conversation!

Coaches who tend to prepare agendas for their meetings must strive to be especially aware of God's activity. They may intend to follow up on insights from a previous session or work through a series of pre-assembled questions. While being prepared for appointments is commendable, coaches must be fully present and sensitive to anything the Holy Spirit desires to accomplish in each encounter. Coaches can easily become so immersed in their own line of questioning that they are oblivious to the Holy Spirit's prompting.

Spiritual presence requires, in coaching terms, the ability to "dance in the moment," to be flexible enough to change direction as needed to pursue what is most important.

Over the years, we have experienced the incredible feeling of being spiritually present with clients. At times, we have seen people experience major breakthroughs. We both immediately realized that God had given them a fresh perspective. On other occasions, the Holy Spirit has prompted us to ask questions we had not previously considered. As soon as the words left our mouth, we recognized that these questions could only have come from God. At such moments, the coaching session often becomes emotional. Yet the coachee fshuld feel loved and accepted, not condemned. Perhaps this sensation is partially what Jesus meant when He said, *"Again, truly I tell you, if two of you on earth agree about any matter that you pray for, it will be done for you by My Father in heaven. For where two or three are gathered together in My name, I am there among them"* (Matt. 18:19-20). Few experiences in life are more powerful than when Christ chooses to reveal Himself as two people earnestly seek Him together.

Third, coaches must eliminate distractions in order to be fully present. Cell phone alerts are a guaranteed disruption. We hope we don't need to say this, but stopping a coaching session to take a call is extremely rude. Coaches might as well look their clients in the face and tell them they are unimportant. My (Bob) phone once rang while I was standing behind the pulpit leading a funeral service. Talk about an unwelcome interruption! We encourage coaches not to set their phone to vibrate either; they should turn it off entirely. Even if they don't answer their phone when it vibrates, they will lose focus in that moment.

Finding a place to meet where there are few disruptions is also important. For example, coaches can certainly conduct sessions over lunch or in coffee shops. For some, this option works well. But these environments are often less conducive to deep, transformative listening. Mundane issues such as hunger or thirst can keep people from being fully present. Coaches should address those needs before meeting with a client.

One final word. Coaches may become distracted by personal issues, such as a sick child or a conflict with a friend. But coaches cannot effectively help others if their mind constantly wanders to their own problems. While entirely compartmentalizing personal thoughts is impossible, coaches should prepare themselves emotionally, spiritually, and physically before each meeting so they can give their full attention to the client.

If coaches are currently battling a personal problem, they may need to heed the apostle Peter's counsel and *"cast all your cares on Him, because He cares about you"* (1 Peter 5:7). At such times, coaches must give their worries to God so they can be an effective instrument in His hands as they coach. They may want to turn Philippians 4:6-7 into a prayer of release:

"I am grateful, dear God, that I have no need to be anxious about anything. Instead, I simply release my concerns to You, including _____. I thank You that You have heard my prayer and will respond in power and love in these situations. Thanks for granting me Your peace. Now please help me give my full attention to _____ and what You are doing in his/her life. Give me Your words and ears that I may be an instrument of Your peace."

Being spiritually present, while not requiring physical presence, does demand mental, emotional, and spiritual availability and focus. People often face difficult issues. They need their coach's full attention.

CONCLUSION

To be effective, coaches must establish redemptive relationships as they build trust by exhibiting authentic, Christ-centered character and being fully present. Coaches must also practice the art of listening attentively on multiple levels. In the next chapter, we will explore four kinds of listening skills.

FOR REFLECTION AND DISCUSSION

1. What aspect of spiritual presence do you most need to improve? What is a skill or behavior you could practice that would communicate that you are fully present with your clients?

2. What most distracts you during conversations with others? What can you do to lessen those distractions?

3. Keep a journal this week of your encounters with people, giving special focus to ways you sense God is working in each person's life during your conversation. You may feel awkward at first, but you will improve as you rely on God and practice this spiritual discipline consistently.

4. Are you currently missing important cues and divine activity as you talk with people? What are you currently failing to notice?

CHAPTER 8

Active, Multi-Level Listening

You're short on ears and long on mouth.
John Wayne

There's a lot of difference between listening and hearing.
G.K. Chesterton

The real heroes anyway aren't the people doing things; the real heroes are the people noticing things, paying attention.
John Green

The human soul yearns to be heard. Being deeply understood is as priceless as it is rare. Social media stands as a not-so-silent testimony to humanity's intense hunger for validation. The coin of the realm in social media is connections and the positive feedback one receives from them. The number of "likes" or

85

"retweets" a post receives reflects the value people place on what the person shared. At times, people all but beg their "friends" to comment on their posts. They might even chastise people if they neglect to do so. Certain social media platforms remind us of loud parties where everyone talks, but no one listens.

The sad reality is that social media does a feeble job meeting humanity's need to feel connected, understood, valued, and affirmed. Those who have developed the capacity to listen well, therefore, are in high demand.

Great listeners are not merely popular; they hold healing in their wings. Rachel Naomi Remen describes this truth:

> Listening is the oldest and perhaps the most powerful tool of healing. It is often through the quality of our listening and not the wisdom of our words that we are able to effect the most profound changes in the people around us.
>
> When we listen, we offer with our attention an opportunity for wholeness. Our listening creates sanctuary for the homeless parts within the other person. That which has been denied, unloved, devalued by themselves and others. That which is hidden.
>
> In this culture the soul and the heart too often go homeless. Listening creates a holy silence. When you listen generously to people, they can hear the truth in themselves, often for the first time.
>
> How does healing occur? It occurs in authentic community, when a person feels deeply understood

and valued by another. There is a reason why solitary confinement is considered such an extreme punishment, and its opposite is also true.[1]

Good listeners connect others to their inner selves and God by modeling compassionate interest. When people do not feel heard, they become alienated, even from their own soul.

In *Hearing God*, Dallas Willard shares his observations of street people in a square near Westminster Cathedral. A homeless woman he saw day after day attracted his attention:

> I recall watching one woman in particular on several occasions as she slept with children and pigeons flocking all around her. . . . While she showed the marks of street life, she looked very much like many a woman at the center of a happy life. And I thought, "Whose daughter is she? Whose sister or mother or neighbor or classmate?" And here she is alone, alone, alone![2]

Effective spiritual coaches foster life transformation as they build redemptive relationships and listen to their clients on multiple levels.

---

[1]Rachel Naomi Remen, *My Grandfather's Blessings* (New York: Riverhead Books, 2001).

[2]Dallas Willard, *Hearing God: Developing a Conversational Relationship With God* (Downers Grove, IL: IVP Press, 2012), 58.

WAYS COACHES LISTEN

1. Before coaches can hear others well, they must give attention to their own inner thoughts.

During a conversation, the listener's own thoughts, worries, and feelings can easily eclipse the speaker's voice. This inner conversation often controls those who are oblivious to it. Though seemingly counter-intuitive, people who want to become better listeners should start by listening to themselves. Which thoughts are intruding on the discussion? Paying attention to self-talk, at least for a time, helps lessen its ability to encroach on a conversation.

Prayer is a powerful means of quieting inner voices. Coaches might begin each session by asking God to silence any disruptive thoughts or concerns. Coaches should acknowledge their own limitations and ask God to help them be fully present. Humility in prayer helps clients focus more intently on God's agenda as well. Those who cannot keep distracting thoughts at bay may miss important details in the conversation.

2. Coaches listen to what is being said.

Too often, people walk away from a conversation without remembering anything the other person said. They were careful to seem interested as they smiled, nodded, or frowned at appropriate moments. They even uttered replies. Truthfully, though, their minds were a thousand miles away!

Ten days after our wedding, my wife, Lisa, and I (Richard) moved 1500 miles to attend seminary. I enrolled in an afternoon Greek class Dr. Tommy Lee taught. On the first day, he asked all 60 students to introduce themselves and share one prayer request. I asked the class to pray for Lisa as she started a new job that week.

Two weeks later, the school held a series of evening services. As Lisa and I were walking toward the auditorium, we happened to pass Dr. Lee. He called me by name, which surprised me since I was one of approximately 200 students he was teaching that semester. Then he noticed my wife.

"Lisa, isn't it?" he asked. Lisa was shocked that he knew her name, since he had never met her. He smiled and asked how her new job was going.

I have never forgotten that conversation. It would have been perfectly excusable for a busy professor to listen half-heartedly as 60 new seminary students shared their prayer concerns. But Dr. Lee had not only listened, he had paid careful attention and remembered. Such listening skills won my unwavering admiration for that professor.

3. Coaches listen "between the lines."

Just as literature students cannot fully understand a poem or novel by focusing solely on the text, coaches are ineffective if they listen only to their client's words. People often communicate subconsciously. *Body language* is one example of nonverbal communication. During the conversation, a client may lean forward and use enthusiastic hand gestures. At other times, the person might turn away from the coach. What prompted that energy shift? Skilled coaches notice even small details. When did he start tapping his hands or feet? What did she communicate by standing up? Why is he sighing? What do these nervous habits indicate? What is stirring within the client's soul?

While teaching at a seminary in Hong Kong, I (Bob) learned about the importance Chinese place on tone of voice. One sound can have eight different meanings in Cantonese depending on the speaker's tone. In English, tone does not usually denote different meanings. Instead, it communicates emotion. As coaches listen to their client, do they hear eager anticipation or reluctance? Compassion or frozen rage? People may say "yes" or "okay," but their tone of voice may undermine their words.

A third "between the lines" noticing skill is the ability to observe the client's use of *metaphors*. The word pictures people paint often hold great emotional power for them. For example, I (Bob) once worked for an organization that treated lower level employees poorly. In a conversation with a top leader, I commented that the organization "ground down" its employees. My word choice conjured up a picture of people passing through a meat grinder. The distorted grimace on the leader's face indicated that the image was as powerful for him as it was for me.

One expression we hear a lot is, "I'm hanging in there!" Unpacking that phrase can be helpful. The coach might ask, "By your fingernails or do you have a firmer grip than that?" Coaches can use the client's own words to open doors to further exploration.

When coaches notice the word pictures or phrases their client uses, they can later reintroduce them in a different form to move the person forward. For example, the image of a lion held unique power for one of my (Bob) clients, especially when he was unsure of himself. It represented the strength and courage he longed to possess. Realizing its importance, I reintroduced this image whenever he took a courageous step: "What a lion you are becoming!" When he needed courage I would say, "Time for the lion within to roar!" I was not simply flattering him. I could sense that God was instilling and calling forth the courage he needed to meet his challenges. At times, coaches might simply repeat their client's metaphors for emphasis, then see how the person responds.

Consider the following metaphors and how a follow-up question might become a springboard for deeper exploration:

- So much is *swirling* around me right now (Which swirling concern needs to be captured first?).
- I've reached my *boiling point* (Who started the fire? What will lower the temperature?).
- Our attendance has *slumped* or *peaked* (How do peaks and valleys impact you spiritually?).

- I feel like I'm *walking on egg shells* (Wow! What is breaking?).
- That guy has been a true *spiritual pillar* in my life (What is he holding up within you?).
- I feel like this *ship is sinking* (Who is in the boat with you?).

By reading between the lines, coaches can notice limiting beliefs their clients hold. For example, a man might say, "I'm stuck in a 'no-win' bind; either my career or my family loses out." The coach might move the conversation from this *either/or* thinking to explore ways he can have *both/and.* A client may say she feels like God abandoned her. The coach might recall Jesus' cry from the cross in Matthew 27:46: *"My God, My God, why have You abandoned Me?"* Then the coach might ask, "Where was the Father and what was He doing at that moment? Where is the Father and what is He doing in your life right now?"

4. Coaches listen spiritually.

Now God has revealed these things to us by the Spirit, since the Spirit searches everything, even the depths of God. For who knows a person's thoughts except his spirit within him? In the same way, no one knows the thoughts of God except the Spirit of God. Now we have not received the spirit of the world, but the Spirit who comes from God, so that we may understand what has been freely given to us by God. We also speak these things, not in words taught by human wisdom, but in those taught by the Spirit, explaining spiritual things to spiritual people. But the person without the Spirit does not receive what comes from God's Spirit, because it is foolishness to him; he is not able to understand it since it is evaluated spiritually (1 Cor. 2:10-14).

To listen spiritually, coaches must utilize the first three listening skills (self-talk, content, between the lines), as well as a fourth skill: noticing uniquely spiritual elements. Coaches must recognize the yearnings within a person's soul that only God can create. For example, only God can draw people to Himself. My (Bob) wife, Teresa, mentored a young woman who was living a wild life. Teresa modeled Christ's unconditional love before her so consistently that an amazing transformation happened. The young woman grew tired of the emptiness she saw in her own lifestyle and longed for spiritual wholeness. A wise coach notices when someone suddenly becomes open to a divine initiative.

Spiritual turning points come in many guises, but God's activity is the common thread. People might experience a growing sense of peace. On the other hand, they may experience a crisis of belief as God calls them to a larger assignment than they can handle alone. During difficult moments, many people only see the pain, not the spiritual opportunity awaiting them. Wise coaches help them find the spiritual promise that is interlaced with their pain. For example, someone may ask, "Why would God do this to me?" The coach might respond, "Why do you think God is refusing to leave you where you are? Could the pain of remaining stagnant ultimately be greater than the pain of moving to a new place?" For more on this subject, see "Chapter Seventeen: Coaching through Seasons of Pain."

Finally, spiritual listening includes the ability to uncover the next steps of faith a person must take. One of Bob's favorite questions is, "What does obedience look like for you right now in this situation?"

One word of caution. Spiritual listening involves both the coach and client. It is a joint-exploration enterprise. It is the client, however, who is ultimately responsible for hearing God's voice. Coaches are only spiritual midwives delivering others into God's presence.

CONCLUSION

Redemptive relationships—forged through trust-building, spiritual presence, and deep-level listening—create an atmosphere for powerful insights to emerge. In the next chapters, we will explore ways coaches can help their clients gain new insights about themselves, God, and their circumstances.

MULTI-LEVEL LISTENING EXERCISES

You can improve your capacity as a listener by practicing these skills with a friend. Here are some conversation starters for each of the four levels.

Level One: Listening to Self

Coachee: Talk about your favorite sports team or TV show.

Coach: Take note of your inner thoughts and feelings as you listen.

Value: Coaches can disempower self-talk by recognizing it and turning their focus toward the other person.

Level Two: Listening to Content

Coachee: Talk about people who have most influenced you and how.

Coach: Try to remember and repeat back everything the coachee said.

Value: This exercise helps improve the coach's ability to remember details.

Level Three: Tone, Body Language, and Metaphors

Coachee: Talk about the type of people who most annoy you.

Coach: Respond with what you noticed about the person's tone of voice and body language. As a higher skill, try to notice the metaphors and other word pictures the person uses.

Value: Enhances the coach's ability to notice visual and auditory cues.

Level Four: Spiritual Listening

Coachee: Talk about the different ways you perceived God as a child, as a young adult, and now.

Coach: Look for spiritual longings, turning points, crises of belief, etc. Use follow-up questions and your own brief observations to probe deeper.

Value: The coach becomes better at noticing what is happening spiritually in the coachee's life.

FOR REFLECTION AND DISCUSSION

1. Which level of listening is the most difficult for you? Why?

2. What might you do to better retain important details people share with you?

3. How might you notice non-verbal messages more effectively? Which non-verbal messages do you tend to miss?

4. How might you better prepare to hear spiritual messages and issues?

Awareness-Raising Skills

Twelve Essential Coaching Skills

META-SKILLS

- Relationship-Building
- **Awareness-Raising**
- Focusing and Commitment
- Futuring

AWARENESS-RAISING META-SKILLS

Helping a person see his or her situation more accurately and clearly through insight-provoking approaches, questions, and messages.

AWARENESS-RAISING SKILLS INCLUDE:

4. Expanding Awareness (Chapter 9)
5. Powerful Spirit-led Questions (Chapter 10)
6. Concise Messages (Chapter 11)

Expanding Awareness

The best way to make dreams come true is to wake up.
Paul Valery

*Self-awareness gives you the capacity to learn from
your mistakes as well as your successes. It enables you
to keep growing.*
Lawrence Bossidy

*If you continue in My word, you really are My disciples.
You will know the truth, and the truth will set you free.*
Jesus (John 8:31-32)

I (Richard) worked with a pastor who was extremely
frustrated by his congregation's resistance to change.
The pastor was a well-educated, good-looking, successful
man, but he was stuck in a winner-take-all battle with
the powers of his church. He was angry at the church
members for lying to him, angry at himself for becoming
their pastor, and angry at God for calling him to the
dysfunctional congregation.

The pastor looked at me grimly and asked what I thought he should do. He was probably expecting me to lead him through a problem-solving exercise or have him take a leadership-style inventory. Instead, I asked a question: "Tell me about how you became a Christian."

He looked puzzled by my seemingly simplistic, irrelevant request. He said he grew up in a dysfunctional home with an alcoholic father. He experienced conflict and disappointment, not joy or affirmation. He became a Christian at a gathering of young adults when he was 18. In that moment, he experienced amazing joy and freedom from his sin and brokenness. Even as he recounted his story, I could see glimmers of that distant joy dart across his face.

"Do you need to become reacquainted with that Jesus?" I asked him. After a moment, he slumped to his knees and cried out to God.

The pastor realized his primary problem was not his church's stubbornness but his heart. He had lost his joy in serving God and leading his flock. He had become more focused on renovating church buildings than facilitating spiritual growth in his people. After momentarily taking his eyes off his problem, he saw the situation much more accurately.

My approach with this man illustrates a distinction between consultants and coaches: *Consultants answer questions. Coaches question answers.* A coach uses questions to puncture self-delusions and bridge gaps in understanding that erode leadership effectiveness. By asking a Spirit-led question, I helped him recognize the core issue.

Thankfully, Immanuel—God with us—does not leave people alone to work out their inner struggles. As people come to know Him intimately, they can see their situation more clearly. Even then, they might battle dark forces and impulses that tear at the soul.

The pastor and theologian Dietrich Bonhoeffer is an inspiration to many. His book *The Cost of Discipleship*, which decries cheap grace, has become a timeless classic. He was imprisoned in Nazi Germany for resisting Hitler and holding firm to the Christian faith. Bonhoeffer was confined first in Buchenwald then at Flossenbürg. He was executed shortly before the Allies liberated the concentration camp in April 1945. Famous for courageously resisting Nazi tyranny and celebrated worldwide for his insightful writing, he nevertheless struggled with his identity while in prison. He faced mortal dangers and indignities each day that degraded his soul. For our age, when social media is an ever-present reminder of the tragic split between people's public and private selves, the poetic letter Bonhoeffer penned to his sister shortly before his execution remains powerfully relevant:

"Who am I?"

Who am I? They often tell me
I would step from my cell's confinement
calmly, cheerfully, firmly,
like a squire from his country-house.

Who am I? They often tell me
I would talk to my warders
freely and friendly and clearly,
as though it were mine to command.

Who am I? They also tell me
I would bear the days of misfortune
equably, smilingly, proudly,
like one accustomed to win.

Am I then really all that which other men tell of?
Or am I only what I know of myself?
restless and longing and sick, like a bird in a cage,
struggling for breath, as though hands were
compressing my throat, yearning for colours,
for flowers, for the voices of birds,
thirsting for words of kindness, for neighborliness,
trembling in expectation of great events,
powerlessly trembling for friends at an infinite
distance,
weary and empty at praying, at thinking, at making,
faint, and ready to say farewell to it all?

Who am I? This or the other?
Am I one person today, and tomorrow another?
Am I both at once? A hypocrite before others,
and before myself a contemptibly woebegone
weakling?
Or is something within me still like a beaten army,
fleeing in disorder from victory already achieved?

Who am I? They mock me, these lonely questions of
mine.
Whoever I am, Thou knowest, O God, I am Thine.[1]

Just as Dietrich Bonhoeffer suffered inner turmoil as
he endured horrific injustices, coaching clients may also
struggle to see a complete picture of themselves and their
challenges. Spiritual coaches help people fully embrace
their authentic, God-given identity. Only then can they
give their "utmost to God's highest purpose."[2] These are
some ways a spiritual coach might help people achieve a
more accurate self-perception:

1. First Steps. When people enlist a coach, they
typically have a specific challenge at the forefront of their
mind. That challenge may be a difficult relationship, a
habit, or a missing skill set that is preventing them from
advancing in their career. One of my (Bob) clients sought
coaching because he had not sensed God's answer to His
prayers for years. A challenge of this nature requires
a deep understanding of the individual before I begin
coaching the problem they present. Many coaches jump
in wherever the person wants to start. But I typically
begin by asking these big-picture questions as I establish
the coaching relationship:

- In a nutshell, what would you most like to get out
  of this coaching relationship?

---

[1]Dietrich Bonhoeffer, "Who am I?" in *Letters & Papers From Prison* (New
York: Touchstone, 1953/1997), 347-8.
[2]Phrase taken from Oswald Chamber's classic devotional book with that title.

- Tell me about yourself, both your public persona and the part of you few people know.
- What are your personal and/or professional goals?
- Tell me about your family and what they desire for you.
- What are your passions?
- What must you accomplish to consider your life satisfying and well lived?
- What do you consider to be your unique calling?
- Tell me how you and God are getting along these days. What would make your relationship better? What else?
- When did you last hear from God, whether through the Bible, prayer, circumstances, or other believers?
- What clear word from God, if any, have you not yet obeyed? Why have you chosen not to obey?

Why do I begin with these questions? Partly to get to know my clients better. Partly to see how the issues they raise in our session fit into their larger life picture. And partly to start expanding their awareness of deeper longings God might be birthing within them.

2. *Spiritual Markers.* Moments in people's life when God clearly speaks to them become spiritual markers. For example, Peter's list of spiritual markers would likely include the moments when Jesus changed his name to Peter (John 1:42), passed by his fishing boat and said, "Follow Me, and I will make you fishers of men" (Matt.4:19), declared, "Upon this rock I will build

My church" (Matt. 16:18), and restored him to service after his shameful denial (John 21:16-19). Peter would also list seeing the resurrected Jesus (Luke 24:28-49) and hearing the Great Commission (Matt 28:18-20) as pivotal moments in his walk with Christ.

SPIRITUAL MARKER EXERCISE

Coaches might use this activity to help clients identify their own spiritual markers:

Identify up to seven times when you believe you encountered God and/or received direction from Him.

- Give each a <u>label</u> (e.g., 8th grade youth camp).
- Provide some <u>context</u> (e.g., I prayed to receive Christ at the close of a service).
- Describe <u>what you heard from and/or learned</u> about God, priorities, yourself, or your calling in this encounter (e.g., I learned the importance of taking a step of faith when circumstances are confusing).

My Spiritual Markers

Marker	Context	What I Learned

Coaches might need to ask probing questions to help people more fully understand these experiences and their continued meaning in their life. Having a chart like this provides some ongoing context to their spiritual journey.

3. Ongoing Awareness-Raising Approaches

A friend of mine (Bob) suffers from retinitis pigmentosa, an eye condition that causes tunnel vision. Most of his peripheral vision is gone, and the center of his vision is blurred. Hemianopsia, another eye condition, causes blindness in one-half of a person's field of vision. Physical conditions such as these can seriously impair one's ability to perform ordinary tasks. In much the same way, people with good physical eyesight can exhibit an emotional or spiritual variant of these conditions. For example, some people might focus intently on a small aspect of their situation and miss the bigger picture. Others may only see half the equation because they fail to consider how those around them view the situation.

Coaches might utilize some of these additional awareness-expanding techniques to help clients better understand their circumstances:

- **Five senses:** Coaches should ask for details about what the person heard, saw, smelled, tasted, or felt in the situation under review. This exercise can fill in important details, especially for "big picture" individuals. For example, one way to sort out reality from hearsay is to ask, "How much of this did you see with your own eyes?"

- **Contrast:** A business leader may say, "I just have to grow this company!" The coach may counter with, "How can you help your company grow big by going small?" Jesus used contrast when He spoke about the tiny mustard seed later dwarfing common herbs when it became a large tree. By using contrast, Jesus helped His listeners understand that, though God's work was starting small, it would multiply into a worldwide movement (Mark 4:30-32).

- **Connect:** Many people lock themselves into a zero-sum mental loop, convinced they must choose between two options. A wise coach may ask them to consider how they might achieve both at the same time.

- **Change perspectives:** A coach might ask, "If I spoke to _____ about this event, how would he/she view it?" or "What do you suppose God thinks about this situation?" The purpose of this technique is to help the individual see the situation from someone else's viewpoint. If the person is married, for example, the coach might ask, "How would your spouse view this situation?" By considering other perspectives, clients can gain fresh insights.

- **Delete:** Coaches might lead clients to imagine how their life would change if a significant element were suddenly removed. For example, if someone prioritizes a job over God, the coach might lead the person to imagine life without that coveted position. What would change? What would stay the same? Coaches might ask an executive who is too busy for his family what his life would be like without them. Such questions, when asked properly, can help the client focus on what truly matters.

- **Death:** God has not promised people a single moment beyond the days that are numbered for them. Psalm 39:4 declares, *"LORD, make me aware of my end and the number of my days so that I will know how short-lived I am."* Most people ignore their own mortality. Nevertheless, major life events—such as a heart attack or the death of a loved one—may compel people to rethink their priorities. At the right time, a good spiritual coach can ask how they might change their life, schedule, or focus if they knew they only had 3-5 years to live.

- **Imagine:** Sometimes it is helpful to imagine someone else joining the conversation. For example, the coachee may be struggling to forgive someone. A coach might say, "Imagine Jesus—with the nail marks visible in His hands—is sitting in that chair next to you. How would you explain to Him the reasons you cannot forgive Jessica?" Or perhaps an executive is trapped by his constant need to make money. The beleaguered businessman may have grown up in a home where his parents argued about finances every evening. For his entire business life, the man might have felt compelled to earn lots of money so he and his family would never face poverty like his father did. A coach could say, "Imagine your father is sitting in that chair, concerned that you are becoming like him. What would you tell him? What do you suppose he might say back to you now?" While the coach must guide such processes carefully, understanding and verbalizing the true issues can help clients address core problems.

Youth ministers pull wild stunts to get their students' attention. One pastor built a Velcro wall and instructed the teenagers to press him against it. Once stuck, he struggled to free himself. In a similar way, people often become stuck in unproductive thought loops. To expand awareness, coaches must engage people's imagination. Using creative methods can be a fun, enlightening way to gain valuable insights.

CONCLUSION

People who seek a coach's help are often intelligent, well-educated people. Yet they can typically only see their problem from a limited viewpoint. They need help to view their situation more clearly. Having a wider perspective does not solve the problem, but it helps people discover new paths that might lead to God's solution. The coach's job is to help clients become free to make informed, God-honoring decisions. Asking powerful, Spirit-led questions is one of the best ways to expand people's awareness. In the next chapter, we will explore what makes a coaching question powerful and effective.

FOR REFLECTION AND DISCUSSION

1. Who in your life is especially good at getting people unstuck? What can you learn from that person?
2. Which of the approaches listed in this chapter would have the greatest impact on you if you were being coached? Why?
3. In Richard's opening story, the pastor thought the issue was resistance to change, but he came to realize that the root cause was spiritual. What might you be missing in a current personal challenge?

CHAPTER 10

Powerful, Spirit-Led Questions

I have no special talents. I am only passionately curious.
Albert Einstein

What people think of as the moment of discovery is
really the discovery of the question.
Jonas Salk

I will also ask you a question. Tell Me. . .
Jesus (Luke 20:3)

John was torn. Should he leave his lucrative position to accept a job at a smaller company thousands of miles away? He was experiencing tremendous success in his career, and he enjoyed living in New York City. He had no reason to change jobs.

Then Steve Jobs asked him one of the most famous questions in the history of business: "Do you want to spend the rest of your life selling sugared water, or do you want a chance to change the world?"[1] After hearing that query, John Scully had his answer. He resigned his position as CEO of Pepsi-Co and become the CEO of Apple Computer.

Powerful questions shake people out of routine thought patterns and make them think more deeply. When guided by the Holy Spirit, a spiritual guide might ask a question that brings a situation into crystal-clear perspective.

Jesus frequently asked transformational questions. A famous example is found in Luke 9. News about Him was spreading like wildfire. Upon entering the district of Caesarea Philippi, Jesus asked His disciples, *"Who are people saying that I am?"* This question was informal and easy to answer.

Following their varied reply, He asked a much more powerful query: *"'But who do you say that I am?' Peter answered, 'God's Messiah'"* (Luke 9:20). Why was this question so impactful? Because, unlike the earlier question, it was deeply personal, open-ended, and called for a response that would have profound implications for their lives. In the subsequent years, Peter reinforced his answer by living so boldly he became one of the earliest Christian martyrs. He was reportedly crucified upside down because he viewed himself unworthy to be executed in the same manner as his Lord. Powerful questions change lives!

---

[1]Walter Isaacson. *Steve Jobs* (New York: Simon and Schuster. 2011), 154.

What makes a coaching question powerful?

- First, powerful coaching questions spring from **genuine curiosity.** The inquirer must sincerely want to learn more about the other person. Know-it-alls fail the curiosity test because, they are consumed by their own viewpoint. The phrase, *"I'm curious. . ."* is a great way to begin a question. For example, I (Bob) occasionally ask leaders experiencing relational challenges this question: "I'm curious. Where else is this issue showing up in your family, friendships, or with other employees?"

- Second, being a **good listener** is a prerequisite to asking powerful questions. Coaches must carefully avoid jumping to conclusions before their client (and God) finishes speaking. Coaches who ask effective questions do not typically say the first thing they think. They ponder what the person said and remain sensitive to the Holy Spirit's prompting. By taking an extra moment to reflect, they are able to select the most powerful question at their disposal. Listening and retention are useful tools for moving people forward. I (Bob) look for patterns in coaching conversations and often ask about possible connections. I might say, "This seems similar to the conflict you had with John a few months ago. How might they be connected?" Or, "What tends to lead you to conflict?" Coaches must listen carefully to determine which line of questioning will be most effective in a particular situation.

- Third, powerful questions are usually **open-ended.** They cannot be answered with a simple yes or no. Instead, they encourage people to give answers that are specific and personal. If coaches only ask questions that require a yes or no answer, clients might feel as though they are being interrogated rather than helped. Here are some yes/no questions that could be improved if they were open-ended:

  - Were you angry with him (*What emotions rose up within you as you spoke with him?*)?
  - Do you know what to do next (*What are some ways you might respond?*)?
  - Have you thought about . . . (*What are your thoughts about . . . ?*)?
  - Do you believe what he said about you (*What credence do you give his comments?*)?
  - Are you committed to taking this step (*How committed are you to taking this step?*)?

Though powerful questions are usually open-ended, one of my (Bob) multi-year coaching relationships began after I asked a simple closed question. An executive recounted example after example of ways a long-term customer kept "letting him down." Out of curiosity, I asked, "Is the future always negative for you?" I am not sure why it popped into my head, but the question led him to see his situation in a new light. Shortly after our conversation, he told me the Lord provided the largest contract in his company's history, as if to remind him the future is not always negative. Powerful questions are usually, but not always, open-ended.

- Fourth, powerful questions are **profoundly relevant** to the person being coached, often touching on deep core values. Coaches should understand their client well enough to discern what questions to ask. Coaches must also be attentive to God's activity in the moment. Jesus' word to Peter echoes the necessity of being spiritually attuned: *"Jesus responded, 'Blessed are you, Simon son of Jonah, because flesh and blood did not reveal this to you, but My Father in heaven'"* (Matt. 16:17). Typically, the problem is not that God is absent, but that people are unaware of His active presence all around them.

The best questions are inspired by God as coaches pray for their clients. The apostle Paul speaks to divine initiatives in 1 Corinthians 2:10-11: *"Now God has revealed these things to us by the Spirit, since the Spirit searches everything, even the depths of God. For who knows a person's thoughts except his spirit within him? In the same way, no one knows the thoughts of God except the Spirit of God."* The role the Holy Spirit plays in the coaching process is what differentiates spiritual leadership coaching from secular coaching. Secular coaches, while helpful in some ways, do not have access to the Holy Spirit. They cannot draw on God's wisdom or resources. The Holy Spirit knows everything about people. He also knows God's plan for the future. When spiritual leadership coaches heed the Holy Spirit's promptings, they may surprise their client with the relevancy and incisiveness of their questions.

At times, coaches may be unsure which direction to take with a client. In those moments, coaches should not be afraid to acknowledge their lack of wisdom and pause the discussion to pray for guidance. They might pray something like this: "Lord, there is a lot going on in Bill's life right now. We clearly have a lot to talk about. We need Your guidance right now so we deal with the issues You know are most important. Please guide our conversation in these next moments. Stopping to pray acknowledges that the Holy Spirit is setting the meeting's agenda.

A few cautions are in order regarding powerful questions. First, if coaches already know the answer the person "should" give to a question they plan to ask, it might be a leading question rather than a powerful one. Leading questions are usually indicative of the coach's agenda for the client and often miss God's agenda by a mile. Using such questions might resemble an interrogation rather than a shared journey.

A second caution concerns *how* coaches ask questions. It is possible to ask a good question in a condescending or condemning manner. Great queries should be delivered in a welcoming, non-judgmental tone of voice.

Remember, the coach's purpose is not to prove a point or win an argument, but to facilitate life-changing insight.

How can coaches determine which questions to ask? First, they should pray for guidance. Second, they should listen carefully and allow the Holy Spirit to lead them. Third, they should consider the communication levels leadership blogger Charlie Gilkey outlined:

- **Social level.** The first level includes subjects such as the weather, sports, news stories, or other interests and hobbies. Communication on this level is superficial, but sometimes a good starting place.
- **Mental level.** The second level focuses on ideas, facts, non-controversial beliefs, plans, strategies, and tips.
- **Emotional level.** The third level includes discussion about wants, needs, aspirations, fears, and joys.
- **Spiritual level.** The highest level transcends the normal "safe" categories of communication and addresses spirituality. For a spiritual leadership coach, this fourth level can be a goldmine of powerful questions.

We would add an "observation level." At this level, coaches might comment on what they observe about their clients during each meeting. Is he dressed more casually than usual? Does she look worried? Did he arrive uncharacteristically early for the meeting? Perhaps the client is carrying a computer bag or something unusual. Did his face flush, eyes widen, or a smile spread across his face when a particular insight dawned on him? Commenting on what appears to be happening can open doors to meaningful, relevant discussion.

In the following pages, we provide two lists of powerful questions. We do not encourage coaches to slavishly follow any set of canned inquiries. But coaches might draw ideas from these questions as they prepare for a conversation. In some ways, providing a list of pre-selected questions betrays the essence of coaching. The best coaches "dance in the moment" and craft questions in real time that raise awareness and promote discovery. Everyone has to begin somewhere, however, and these questions can assist new coaches and add to seasoned coaches' tool kit. With practice, coaches will develop their own unique set of coaching questions, while remaining open to questions that arise in the moment.

POWERFUL COACHING QUESTIONS FOR EACH META-SKILL

Relationship

- What should I know about you that will help me coach you well?
- What have previous coaches, mentors, or friends done that has brought out the best in you?
- What is on your mind today? What would make things better?
- What do you most hope to gain from our time together?
- How will you know when you have achieved that goal? What are the measurables?

Awareness

- What have you tried so far? How well has that worked?
- What are some other options you have considered? What else?
- *For either/or thinking:* What are some ways to achieve/do both?
- Who do you know who can help you with this? Who else?
- What do you need to *be* and *do* to succeed?
- What would success/faithfulness look like in this situation?
- What have you learned from similar challenges or experiences that can help you in this situation?
- Oh, really?
- What is God's still small voice saying to you right now?

Focus and Commitment

- What do you most want (to happen)? Not want (to happen)?
- Progress on which of these situations/challenges would have the greatest positive impact on your life?
- What can you control/influence in this situation, and what is beyond your control/influence?
- If you were coaching me in this situation, what advice would you give?
- What do you sense God wants you to do?

- *For "I don't know" responses:* What is your hunch?
- What commitment will you make today? Anything else?
- What will you do by when?
- On a scale of 1-10, how committed are you to taking these steps?

Futuring

- How will (your life, work, relationships, situation) be better as a result of success in this area?
- Once you have achieved this goal, how and what will you feel?
- What do you need to do or who might you enlist to keep you on track?
- What might go wrong? What will you do then? What is your Plan B?
- What has stood out to you during this session? What are some of your takeaways?
- *Review:* So what will you do by when?

POWERFUL SPIRIT-LED QUESTIONS AND THE SEVEN REALITIES

The best questions come from God, not a list. But the questions below may reveal God's work in a person's life.

1. **God is always at work around you.**

   - Tell me about some times when you know God encountered you (It may be helpful for people to develop a list of up to seven instances, the context of each, and what they learned about God through those experiences.).

- When is the last time you felt God working in your life?
- What do you sense God is doing right now in the lives of people around you?

2. **God pursues a continuing love relationship with you that is real and personal.**

   - When did God become more than a doctrine or concept to you?
   - What are some ways you feel God is pursuing (or hounding) you?
   - When have you felt God's love most? Least?

3. **God invites you to become involved with Him in His work.**

   - How would you describe your personal calling?
   - What is the one thing you simply *must* do in life?
   - In what ways have you recently sensed an unusual stirring or spiritual hunger in people who are not normally spiritually interested?
   - What are the areas of spiritual restlessness within your soul? What might the Holy Spirit be preparing you to do or become?

4. **God speaks by the Holy Spirit through the Bible, prayer, circumstances, and the church to reveal Himself, His purposes, and His ways.**

    - How have you sensed God speaking to you as you prayed and read His Word?
    - What passage in the Bible has significantly impacted you lately?
    - What unusual circumstances have you experienced recently? How do you sense God might be working in or through them?
    - What have other people said to you that seems to have the ring of truth or conviction?
    - What have you learned lately about God and His ways?

5. **God's invitation for you to work with Him always leads you to a crisis of belief that requires faith and action.**

    - What is the biggest challenge for you right now?
    - What is the last thing you know God asked you to do that you have not yet obeyed?
    - What do you most fear in this situation?
    - In what ways is God calling you into deep waters in this situation?

6. **You must make major adjustments in your life to join God in what He is doing.**

    - What does obedience look like in this situation?
    - What will you do?

- Which of these choices most clearly reflects God's character? Which choice requires you to trust God more?
- How open are you to making the necessary changes?

7. **You come to know God by experience as you obey Him and He accomplishes His work through you.**

  - How has God worked through you lately?
  - When has obedience led to real blessing or growth in your life?
  - In what aspect of your life do you most feel the pleasure or power of God?
  - How has God been more "real" to you lately than He has seemed before?

CONCLUSION

Questions are one of the most effective and powerful tools in a coach's tool kit. Coaches should not become complacent with their ability to ask questions. There is always room for improvement! Nevertheless, questions alone do not always lead to necessary change. At times, a more direct approach is necessary. In the next chapter, we will explore "Concise Messages."

FOR REFLECTION AND DISCUSSION

1. What makes a question powerful? What makes it spiritually powerful?
2. Review the questions contained in this chapter and elsewhere throughout the book. From these,

compile a single-page cheat sheet of powerful questions you might fruitfully employ. Do not go through each question sequentially, but rather learn them well enough that they will naturally come to mind at the right moment to meet a particular need.

3. Enlist some people who will allow you to coach them around a topic of their choosing, perhaps in an area of their life where they feel "stuck." Practice using some of these questions as you coach them. Get feedback from them about which questions helped them the most.

4. What are three ways you could make your question-asking more powerful and effective?

CHAPTER 11

Concise Messages

*The most valuable of all talents is that of never using
two words when one will do.*
Thomas Jefferson

*Men occasionally stumble over the truth, but most of
them pick themselves up and hurry off as if nothing
ever happened.*
Winston Churchill

When Richard and I (Bob) co-teach leadership
seminars, I lead a segment on team-building and
communication. As an exercise, we play a game called
"Nuclear Waste." The object of the game is simple: the
team must pick up a rope contraption, take it to a second
location, expand it around a large can filled with water
(nuclear waste), then use the device to carry the can to
a safe spot without spilling any liquid death along the
way. Easy, right? Not exactly. Seven team members are
blindfolded, and the designated leader—the only person

who can see—may only use vocal instructions to guide them.

On one occasion, the leader doled out a string of complex and confusing instructions to his bewildered charges:

"Take two steps to the right, then three steps forward."
"Who, me?"
"No, I meant John. Back up!"
"Who?"

After twenty minutes of collective vexation, I stopped the game early to discuss what went wrong. The leader had failed to use simple commands, such as "follow my voice."

The leader of a different group never explained the objective of the game to his team. He simply led his sightless compatriots down a series of stairs into a corridor and then asked, "What do you all want to do?" Exasperated groans echoed down the hallway! Both leaders failed to communicate clearly and compellingly enough to move their team to success.

People periodically find themselves stuck in a pattern of circular reasoning, wishful thinking, or denial. Great coaches know that people sometimes need a wake-up call to jolt them into seeing reality. On those occasions, a coach's best tool may be a concise message. Master coach Jane Creswell describes a concise message as typically consisting of the following:

- *Seven or fewer words*

- *Followed by silence*[1]

We would add that concise messages should be deeply relevant to the individual, touching on the person's core values.

When getting someone's attention, less is more. Jesus knew that a brief word could change lives, and He was a master of the concise message. Consider these examples:

- *Come and see* (John 1:39).
- *You still lack one thing* (Luke 18:22).
- *Go, call your husband* (John 4:16).
- *What is that to you* (John 21:22)?
- *Let the dead bury their own dead* (Luke 9:60).
- *Do not be unbelieving, but believing* (1 John 20:27).
- *Do you want to be made well* (John 5:6)?

The prophet Nathan demonstrated the power of a concise message when he confronted King David after the monarch committed adultery with Bathsheba and had her husband murdered. Nathan told David a story about a powerful, wealthy man who took and killed a poor man's lone ewe lamb. When David heard the story, he became enraged and blurted out, *"As the LORD lives, the man who did this deserves to die! Because he has done this thing and shown no pity, he must pay four lambs for that lamb"* (2 Sam. 12:5-6). Nathan responded with a concise message that cut David to the quick: *"You are*

---

[1] For more information about Jane Creswell and the coach training process she developed, visit https://getpositive.today/get-positive-coach-training/.

that man" (2 Samuel 12:7). Four simple words instantly humbled the greatest man in the land.

Coaches sometimes work with clients who are long on talk but short on action. These people pay coaches top dollar to listen to their prejudices, biases, opinions, and excuses. But they have no genuine intent to change.

I (Bob) coached a pastor who frequently broke his personal commitments. Finally, realizing this client was not doing himself or his church members any good, I ended the session with this concise message: "Let's coach again when you're ready." He immediately understood that our coaching relationship had ended. He was shocked that I, the paid coach, was unwilling to listen to him make endless excuses. A year later, I learned that he had taken the concise message as a wake-up call to get serious about the promises he had made to himself and God.

I (Richard) was a seminary president for 13 years. During my tenure at the school, I often met with students individually. One day I spoke with a young man who was experiencing numerous conflicts with classmates. As we talked about these quarrels, the man repeatedly blamed others. His excuses grew to the point of absurdity as he refused to accept responsibility for any of the disputes. I finally commented, "Always being blameless is mathematically impossible!" Then I remained silent. I knew he was clinging to a false version of reality and needed someone to help him see another perspective. I did not say everything was his fault; I simply suggested that no one could experience the number of interpersonal conflicts he had and remain faultless.

Concise messages are powerful because they are clear and direct. Some coaches love talking so much they obscure profound truths with unnecessary comments. In contrast, the starkness of a concise message produces a "Whoa!" moment. When the coach needs to challenge a false assumption, the message can be as simple as a raised eyebrow accompanied by, "Oh, really?"

After delivering such a word, coaches should remain silent and allow the person to feel the statement's full impact. If their message appears to have had a strong effect, coaches may be tempted to soften the blow. But they should resist the urge to speak. Instead, they should let the ensuing silence do the heavy lifting.

Concise messages can have a positive focus. I (Bob) coached a successful pastor who failed to embrace his God-given worth. Year after year, peers and denominational decision makers selected him for increasingly significant positions. During one coaching session, the Holy Spirit guided me to utter four words that helped the man embrace his true value and giftedness: "You keep being chosen!" Those words, delivered at just the right time, shattered the man's distorted view of himself. The pastor had seen himself as unworthy, but my concise statement offered compelling evidence to the contrary.

We would like to offer a couple of cautions regarding concise messages. First, coaches should use them sparingly. A coach with a strong personality may fire off a steady stream of zingers that do more damage than good. Such statements can have a jarring, even numbing effect. If coaches use them too often, the client might feel embattled, humiliated, and defeated.

Second, coaches should use concise messages only for a redemptive purpose. Why? Because a concise message can either be a catalyst for positive change or lead to a life sentence of self-doubt. I (Bob) served as a voluntary student missionary for ten weeks one summer while in college. During that time, I met a pastor (I will call him Bill) who recounted a painful encounter he had in seminary a decade earlier. When Bill and a friend sat down for lunch in the cafeteria, a professor they both respected joined them. The professor commenced to gush praise on his friend, declaring that he could see the man's great ministerial promise. He then made clear, in a few dismissive words, that he saw far less ministry potential for Bill. The professor extended a blessing to Bill's friend, but left Bill feeling as if he had been cursed. Years after the incident, Bill was still emotionally shackled by that uncaring comment. Words have power to bless or curse. Coaches should always use them carefully and prayerfully!

Employing a concise message effectively hinges on timing, brevity, delivery, and incisiveness. Coaches should not use a concise message early in a conversation. Instead, they should hold it in reserve. If, however, the coach's questions have not succeeded in leading the person to genuine self-discovery, a more direct approach might be necessary.

Coaches should take the following steps when delivering a short message: First, they should mull over their word choice. Second, they should make sure their message is as concise as possible. Third, they should be mindful of their delivery. Coaches should not act antagonistic or threatening, but they ought to appear confident. If they utter the concise message in a faltering, quiet, uncertain tone, their words will not have a powerful impact. Finally, they should ensure their message is incisive. That is, it must cut straight to the heart of the issue. If coaches make a concise statement about a secondary or tertiary issue, its effect will be largely lost.

We hesitate to offer specific suggestions at this point, because these statements are extremely dependent on the moment, circumstance, person, and tone of the preceding conversation. We do not encourage coaches to employ these exact statements in their practice. But for illustrative purposes, here are some examples of concise messages:

- "Your story sounds like a Shakespearian Tragedy" (*Repetitious stories of woe*)!
- "And you did that in love, right" (*Mixed motives*)?
- "Being perfect must be a great burden" (*Unwillingness to admit fault*)!
- "You give feedback better than you receive it" (*Unteachable spirit*).

- "So why do you need a coach" (*No desire to grow or change*)?
- "And she didn't appreciate your candor" (*Wounding others*)?
- "It seems like we've traveled this road before . . ." (*Patterns of thought, behavior*).

Each of these statements, delivered at the right moment and in the proper manner, can exert a big impact.

Coaches might also repeat people's own words back them to powerful effect. For example, a client might declare, "I did nothing wrong!" As the coach asks probing questions, however, the client may disclose various ways his words and actions contributed to the problem. At a key moment, the coach could look the client in the eye and say, questioningly, "I did nothing wrong?" At times, the most convicting, disarming, troublesome words people can hear are their own.

Delivering a concise message successfully requires discernment. Ecclesiastes 3:1 declares that there is a proper time for every activity under heaven. To be effective, the message must be concise, pointed, relevant, thought-provoking, and delivered at exactly the right moment. For that, coaches must walk in step with the Spirit.

CONCLUSION

When coaches use powerful, Spirit-led questions and concise messages, they lead people to a higher level of understanding. New insights become springboards to meaningful commitments. In the next chapter, we will explore ways coaches can help people become focused and committed to taking the best steps forward.

FOR FURTHER REFLECTION AND DISCUSSION

1. When has a concise message set you free? What was the message?
2. When has a misguided concise message harmed you?
3. What keeps you from remaining silent after you make a concise statement?
4. How can you trim the number of words you use so they are more decisive?

Focusing and Commitment Skills

Twelve Essential Coaching Skills

META-SKILLS

- Relationship-Building Skills
- Awareness-Raising Skills
- **Focusing and Commitment Skills**
- FuturingSkills

META-SKILL THREE: FOCUSING AND COMMITMENT SKILLS

Leading an individual to take concrete steps to accomplish God's purpose in his or her life.

FOCUS AND COMMITMENT SKILLS INCLUDE:

7. Narrowing the Focus (Chapter 12)
8. Calling for Commitment (Chapter 13)
9. Chosen Accountability (Chapter 14)

Narrowing the Focus

To be everywhere is to be nowhere.
Seneca

Being selective—doing less—is the path of the productive.
Focus on the important few and ignore the rest.
Timothy Ferriss

Children of our generation passed countless hours on playground merry-go-rounds. We thrilled at the sensation of the wind on our faces as we sped around and around. But I (Bob) also remember finding myself at the mercy of older kids who demonstrated an abject lack of mercy as they commandeered the turnabout. The bullies would spin us faster and faster and then dare us to jump off at top speed. We were all but guaranteed to skin some unfortunate part of our body—hands, knees, face, or shoulder—and spend the evening wincing with each step.

Spinning in circles is enjoyable for children, but disastrous for adults striving to fulfill their divine purpose. Well-intentioned initiatives can easily become sidelined by distractions, competing priorities, and petty urgencies. A wise coach knows how to untangle swirling thoughts and guide the conversation in a fruitful direction.

The coach should begin a session by listening carefully to the client's concerns. As a neutral but caring person, the coach may then lead the client to identify the primary issues at hand. Certain schools of thought in the counseling world purport that people gain relief simply by talking about problems. Spiritual leadership coaches, however, do not merely allow people to vent or express frustration. They help people *resolve* issues so they can move forward and fulfill their divine calling. Coaches help people achieve resolution by guiding them to focus on one coachable issue at a time.

What makes an issue coachable? In *7 Habits of Highly Effective People*, Steven Covey identifies two concentric circles. The larger circle, which he labeled the *"Circle of Concern,"* represents anything that might worry people: their job, crime, the possibility of war, aging, and the like. He labeled the much smaller inside circle the *"Circle of Influence."*[1]

Covey claims that successful people focus only on matters they can control or influence. As they successfully give attention to those issues, their "Circle of Influence"

---

[1] Stephen R Covey, *The 7 Habits of Highly Effective People: Powerful Lessons in Personal Change* (New York: Simon and Schuster, 2013), 87-92.

tends to expand. Fixating on issues outside one's control is futile. A coachable issue, then, is a problem a person can take positive steps toward solving.

Jesus addressed a similar spiritual principle when he told the parable of the talents. He ended the story with this conclusion: *"I tell you, that to everyone who has, more will be given; and from the one who does not have, even what he does have will be taken away"* (Luke 19:26). Jesus was speaking about faithfulness. The master did not judge the servant by factors outside his control. Rather, he was accountable for what had been entrusted to him.

I (Richard) recall speaking with a man who had become extremely discouraged by the nation's political and social condition. He vented his frustrations on social media and castigated those who disagreed with his opinion. He confessed that he spent between two and three hours watching the news each day.

"How is watching the news affecting you?" I inquired. He said it was making him angry.

"And how is watching the news solving any of the problems you are learning about?" I asked. He sheepishly admitted that his news-watching was not making the world better in any way.

I then questioned him about his responsibilities in his family, job, and church. Could he be more effective in those spheres of influence? He acknowledged that he had many unfulfilled goals in those areas. I asked why he had not achieved them.

"Lack of time," he responded immediately. As soon as the words left his mouth, the light came on! He realized he had become so consumed with matters he could not change that he had neglected important issues within his sphere of influence. His life had become dangerously distracted.

Neuroscientist John Ratey explains that individuals who are unable to filter out non-essential stimuli become frozen by over-stimulation.[2] The same principle is true in the spiritual realm. One of the most nefarious tactics the evil one employs is distraction. A thousand petty urgencies crowd out issues of singular importance.

Coaches can use the following method to help clients achieve focus:

- *Begin the discussion with a focus question.* Here are some variations:

  - "What dilemma could we solve today that would mean the most to you (or make the greatest difference in your life or work)?"
  - "What is keeping you up at night these days?"
  - For the financially motivated, a coach might ask, "What single issue, if we made substantial progress on it today, would make the time and money you invested in this session worthwhile?"
  - Or the coach could simply ask, "What would you like to coach around today?"

---

[2]John Ratey, *A User's Guide to the Brain* (New York: Vintage, 2002). See Chapter 3, "Attention and Consciousness."

- *Recap and Refocus.* During some coaching conversations, the client may mention concern after concern without making any movement toward resolution. In those situations, coaches should ask a refocus question. Here are some possibilities:

"We have talked about a, b, and c . . ."

  - "Of these three issues, which is the most important one to work on today?"
  - "Which one issue, if we solved it today, would make the others easier to resolve?"
  - "Which of these issues are beyond your control, and which ones are within your control?"
  - "Which of these problems most breaks your heart?"
  - "What is the one thing you could do that would make the biggest difference?"
  - "Which one of these issues matters the most to you right now? To your long-term goals? To God?"
  - "Is this an issue we can park for a while until we have resolved more pressing concerns?"
  - "Okay. We haven't resolved the previous issue yet. Do you want to move on to this new concern now, or should we stick with the original problem?"
  - "Wait, wait, wait! We haven't established our target yet!

I (Richard) worked with a woman who had both dyslexia and ADHD. She simply could not process information in a linear fashion. Our conversations were derailed by every new thought that entered her head. Unsurprisingly, this woman was overwhelmed by numerous unresolved issues in her life.

I policed our conversations. Every time she brought up an extraneous topic, I would say, "Well we may need to get to that, but we have not put the other matter to bed yet. Let's stick with that." And we would return. This woman's mind did not work in straight lines, and no one had ever helped her stay with one issue until it was resolved. As a result, her life was cluttered with unsolved problems that overwhelmed her. In truth, only a handful of those problems were serious. But they were buried in a sea of extraneous, non-essential concerns that constantly distracted her.

COACHING MODELS TO FOCUS THE CONVERSATION

Some coaches use specific coaching models to keep their conversations moving forward. Frankly, there are almost as many coaching models available as there are coaching organizations. The following three methods can help guide a coaching conversation in a focused, fruitful direction.

GROW Model

- GOAL—What do you want?
- REALITY—What is happening now?

- OPTIONS—What could you do?
- WILL—What will you do?[3]

The value of this model, popular in management and coaching circles, is that it is simple and easy to memorize. It encourages the individual to consider available options and then commit to take steps toward achieving the goal. As a value-neutral model, it begins with the client's desire. As such, it leaves God and Christian values out of the equation.

Collaborative Conversation Model

- **Establish FOCUS**—What are the intended outcomes?
- **Discover POSSIBILITIES**—Identify insights and options for moving forward.
- **Plan the ACTIONS**—Assign responsibility for each task.
- **Remove BARRIERS**—Identify potential obstacles and plan workarounds.
- **REVIEW**—Who will do what by when?[4]

Two new dynamics contained in this model are Barriers and Review. An effective coach should explore what might go wrong and what workarounds to consider if necessary (See Chapter 15). This model, not being an acronym, is more difficult to remember during a coaching conversation. It is also faith-neutral, so God is not an integral part of the process.

---

[3] To learn more about the GROW model, go to
https://www.performanceconsultants.com/grow-model.
[4] See www.coachworks.com for the Collaborative Conversation Model.

4D FLOW Approach[5]

- **Discern**—Where is God working?
- **Discover**—How does He want me to participate?
- **Develop**—What are the next steps?
- **Depend**—Whom do I need?

Without God, people go astray. Their desires are skewed by their own sinful passions, and their plans become self-centered. By discerning God's activity at the beginning of the conversation, clients are prepared to align the plan with His will rather than their own ambitions or struggles.

OUR CAUTION

Each of these models is valuable. Beware, though, of the temptation to rely on a model rather than on the Holy Spirit's guidance. Think of these models as training wheels. They represent the science side of coaching. But coaching is also a spiritual art. Coaches must be attuned to God and ready to change their approach in obedience to His prompting.

CAN'T I SOMETIMES JUST GIVE ADVICE?

A coach approach does not normally include advice-giving. But it is sometimes helpful for the coach to brainstorm with the client. The coach may even offer ideas or suggestions. On such occasions, I (Bob) have said, "Do you mind if I take off my coach hat for a

---

[5]The 4D Flow Model is detailed in Steve Ogne and Time Roehl *TransforMissional Coaching: Empowering Leaders in a Changing Ministry World* (Nashville, B&H Books, 2008), 115.

moment and make a recommendation?" Or, "Can I be a pastor with you for just a moment?" Coaches should use this method sparingly. If they dole out advice frequently, they might be serving their own interests or presenting answers clients should discover for themselves.

CONCLUSION

By guiding clients to focus on a single coachable issue, the coach helps them sort out priorities, narrow their focus, and channel their life in a more fruitful direction. The next step is two-fold: remaining focused on the topic they chose and exploring the focus area in greater depth until they are ready to take concrete steps forward.

FOR REFLECTION AND DISCUSSION

1. As you consider ways to improve as a coach, what is within and what is outside your control?
2. Which two refocus questions do you consider most powerful? Why?
3. Which of the coaching models seems to fit you best? Why?

CHAPTER 13

Calling for Commitment

The most difficult thing is the decision to act. The rest is merely tenacity.
Amelia Earhart

What are you prepared to do?
Malone to Elliot Ness in *The Untouchables*

The beloved children's book *But Who Will Bell the Cat?* spins a tale about a group of mice that is concerned about the dreaded house cat. During a particularly vexing brainstorming session, a mouse comes forward with a brilliant idea: "Let's place a bell on the cat so we can always know when the cat is nearby!" The rodent gathering erupts with excited shouts of approval, until one wise old mouse asks the critically important question, "But who will bell the cat?"

A great gulf exists between ideas and commitments. People can discuss ideas until the cows come home without ever making a decision. Effective spiritual leadership coaches ask hard questions that lead to solid commitments. Tom Landry, famed former coach of the Dallas Cowboys, described his job this way: "I make men do what they don't want to do, so they can become the players they always wanted to be." Landry sagely understood that, though people generally desire success, they sometimes need encouragement to choose the path that leads to positive results.

In reality, it is extremely difficult for people to keep life-changing commitments in their own strength. God must take the lead role in shaping His children into Christ's image through various life experiences (Rom. 8:28-29). Spiritual leadership coaches join God's inner work through powerful Spirit-led questions that lead to spiritual commitments, not just religious sentiments.

How do coaches lead their client to make and keep spiritual commitments? They challenge the person to do the following:

- Make a specific commitment.
- Within a set time frame.
- That is directly related to God's revealed purpose for the person.

Commitments should be clearly defined. For example, a man might say he needs to become a better husband. But his statement does not include any criteria for what being a better husband entails or how he plans to become one. The gap between "I need to" and "I commit to" is huge! When a man pledges to give his wife a daily compliment, help with the dishes after every meal, and take out the garbage without being asked, however, he has promised something that is clear and measurable.

Another factor to consider is spiritual relevance. Does the goal align with God's revealed purpose? People can easily become excited about good things that are not God's best for them. People can mistakenly pursue secondary goals while neglecting primary issues. Clarity and focus are the best defense against the enemy's tactics of confusion and diversion.

The prophet Elijah is a great example of someone who called God's people to make a specific and timely commitment. King Ahab, under the influence of his wife, Jezebel, led Israel toward idolatrous Baal worship. At Mount Carmel, Elijah called God's people to take a clear stand:

> Then Elijah approached all the people and said, "How long will you waver between two opinions? If the LORD is God, follow him. But if Baal, follow him." But the people didn't answer him a word (1 Kings 18:21-22).

God's people kept hedging their bets, vacillating between serving the Lord and worshiping Baal depending on which was more convenient at the time. But Elijah's historic showdown between good and evil forced them to make a lasting commitment.

Likewise, I (Bob) have noticed that my clients often use language that allows "wiggle room." In reality, using generalities is a way of avoiding commitments. Perceptive coaches pay attention to words and, when appropriate, call out fuzzy terminology. For example, I sometimes ask clients one of these commitment questions:

- What changes do you need to make in your life based on our conversation today?
- What specific actions will you take to achieve your aim?
- So, what will you do by when?
- So, what are your specific commitments from today?

The client often replies with a vague, "Well, I need to do such and such." I may counter by stating, "I listen carefully to words, and I find that there is a huge gap between 'need to' and 'going to.' What are you willing to commit to do?"

The following dialogue is an example of successful focusing and commitment-making conversation:

Coach: So, you have determined that God wants you to set a more Christ-like example for your employees?
Coachee: That's right. I want them to see Jesus in me!
Coach: How will you do that?
Coachee: I need to start by treating them better.
Coach: How so? What will you do differently?
Coachee: I need to show them I care.
Coach: What will you do to show them you care?
Coachee: Maybe I can ask them more about their personal and family life.

Coach: So you have thirty employees. What is a reasonable, measurable goal for you to make daily or weekly?

Coachee: I can start files on my employees to keep track of birthdays, names of family members, and concerns they have mentioned so I can ask focused questions that show them I care.

Coach: That's great! When will you complete the files?

Coachee: I will develop the form and have my assistant create a file for each employee by the end of next week.

Coach: How frequently will you review the files and have these conversations?

Coachee: I will normally review one file and check in on at least one person per day. During crunch times, I will do at least three per week.

Coach: When will you begin?

Coachee: This Monday morning.

Coach: That's great! May I suggest one addition?

Coachee: Sure. What's that?

Coach: Have your assistant place the file on your desk each day so you don't forget. And take time to pray specifically for the employee before each conversation.

Coachee: Thanks. I'll do that!

Notice how the coach guided the conversation from fuzzy intentions to focused commitments. Coaches must not be afraid to ask hard questions in order to move their client from generalized sentiments to specific actions. Patient perseverance is key! Coaching is never simply about changed perspectives. Effective coaching always leads to changed behavior.

Coaches should make sure their client's goals contain the following components: First, the commitment should include *specific actions*. Rather than making vague statements, such as, "I need to spend more time at home," coaches should encourage clients to identify specific actions they plan to take, such as, "I am going to resign from the school board next week so I can spend Monday evenings at home with my family." People cannot solve a problem until they commit to a specific plan of action. Bossidy and Charan, in *Execution*, explain: "Unless you translate big thoughts into concrete steps for action, they're pointless. Without execution, the breakthrough thinking breaks down, learning adds no value, people don't meet their stretch goals, and the revolution stops dead in its tracks."[1] Coaches help their clients transform their dreams into action.

Second, the commitment should include *timing*. If a client says, "I will try to spend more time with my three teenage children," the coach should continue to probe until the client sets a deadline. Perhaps the coach ultimately leads the client to make this commitment: "Before this weekend, I will make a date with each of my kids to meet for a one-on-one lunch within the next thirty days." The client's goal now includes a specific plan of action as well as a timeline.

---

[1] Larry Bossidy, Ram Charran, and Charles Burck, *Execution: The Discipline of Getting Things Done* (New York: Random House Publishers, 2002), 12.

Third, the commitment should include *measurable goals*. A person might say, "I need to care more about my employees." The individual's sentiment is noble, but measuring a person's heart is difficult! The person would be better off making a quantifiable commitment: "I am going to give my employees a gift certificate this month, with a note of appreciation for their efforts." The individual's commitment is now measurable.

Coaches must help people sustain hope as they work to keep commitments. One client I (Bob) coached had skillfully led his team to success throughout his long and storied career. He grew despondent, however, by his inability to accomplish an important personal goal. To help him sustain hope, we worked together to identify specific actions he needed to take to achieve victory. We prioritized critical steps. Then I asked him to determine which tasks he needed to complete himself and which ones he could delegate to others. I invited him to build a team that would help him accomplish the task. Lastly, I asked him to commit to taking the necessary steps to achieve success. Once we broke his big task into measurable actions, the problem no longer appeared insurmountable. I also guided him to reflect on wisdom he had gained from facing similar challenges in the past. As a result, his venture ended in success and he regained his confidence.

CONCLUSION

Tangible commitments provide a great starting point, but they do not guarantee a successful outcome. To bring ideas into reality, accountability and futuring skills are required.

FOR REFLECTION AND DISCUSSION

1. When asked for a commitment, what might cause a person to be vague in their response?

2. What spiritual dynamics are occurring as a person being coached struggles to make clear commitments?

3. In what ways is "the devil in the details"?

4. What commitment to God are you presently putting off?

CHAPTER 14

Chosen Accountability

He that is good for making excuses is seldom good for anything else.
Benjamin Franklin

But be doers of the word and not hearers only, deceiving yourselves.
James 1:22

Iron sharpens iron, and one person sharpens another.
Proverbs 27:17

Jesus was a master storyteller. In one narrative, He spoke about a man who told his two sons to work in the fields. The first son refused, but later changed his mind and went. The second son promised to go, but never did (Matt. 21:28-32). Jesus clearly explained that acknowledging a need is not enough. Making commitments is insufficient. There is no substitute for action!

THE CHALLENGE OF ACCOUNTABILITY

Accountability to God, oneself, and others is important, because people have a sinful tendency to avoid taking responsibility for their failure. After Adam was tricked into eating the forbidden fruit in the Garden of Eden, he blamed his wife! Eve accused the serpent (Gen. 3:12-13). Adam and Eve were not unusual in that regard. People often attempt to escape personal accountability by blaming others—perhaps even their coach! In *Winning with People*, John Maxwell illustrates people's tendency to evade responsibility this way:

Cliff, while flying in a hot air balloon, realized he was lost. He reduced his altitude and spotted a woman below. He descended a bit more and shouted, "Excuse me, can you help me? I promised a friend I would meet him an hour ago, but I don't know where I am." The woman below replied, "You are in a hot air balloon, hovering approximately 30 feet above the ground. You are between forty and forty-one degrees north latitude and between fifty-nine and sixty degrees west longitude."

"You must be an engineer," said the balloonist. "I am," replied the woman, "How did you know?" "Well," answered the balloonist, "Everything you told me is technically correct, but I have no idea of what to make of your information, and the fact is that I am still lost. Frankly, you've not been much help so far."

The woman below responded, "You must be in management." "I am," replied the balloonist. "But how did you know?" "Well," said the woman, "you don't know where you are or where you are going. You have risen where you are due to a large quantity of hot air. You made a promise which you have no idea how to keep. And you expect people beneath you to solve your problems. The fact is you are in exactly the same position you were in before we met, but now, somehow, it's my fault."

Coaches best serve their clients when they help them see their situation clearly, develop their own action plan for success, and make a personal commitment to take those actions. Though their role is important, coaches should keep responsibility for success or failure where it belongs—with the coachee. If the coach is not careful, external motivators for ensuring compliance—such as guilt, fear, nagging, and cajoling—can become a ticking time-bomb within the person. They may produce short-term acquiescence, while setting in motion an internal, long-term resistance that sabotages the intended results.[1]

Sports and corporate psychologist Jim Taylor writes that the deepest and longest-lasting motivators emanate from within. In his Motivation Matrix, he measures motivation along two dimensions: internal vs. external and positive vs. negative.[2] Motivations that fall within

---

[1]For more on this, see Em Griffith, *Mindchangers: The Art of Christian Persuasion* (Carol Stream, IL: Tyndale, 1977), 45.

[2]*Psycholgy Today*, https://www.psychologytoday.com/blog/the-power-prime/201201/personal-growth-motivation-the-drive-change (Accessed August 28, 2017).

each of the resulting four quadrants typically produce different experiences and outcomes.

MOTIVATION MATRIX

	Internal	External
Positive	**Motivators:** Passion, self-validation, challenge, satisfaction, desire **Outcome:** Successful, fulfilled and happy	**Motivators:** Financial rewards, security, professional recognition and appreciation **Outcome:** Some success, mostly fulfilled, but dependent on others for continued feelings of success
Negative	**Motivators:** Fear of failure, feelings of inadequacy, insecurity **Outcome:** Considerable success, but a high rate of burnout and general unhappiness even after success is attained	**Motivators:** Pressure from significant others, unstable life, financial pressure **Outcome:** Some success, yet continued feelings of anxiety and unhappiness even after success is attained

THE KEY: ENHANCING INTRINSIC MOTIVATION

As the preceding chart demonstrates, Positive Internal Motivation produces the greatest long-term results. Here are some internal motivators coaches can use as springboards for perseverance and positive change:

- *Identity in Christ.* In the Bible, people's names described their personal identity. When God encountered individuals in a significant way, He sometimes changed their names to reflect their new character or status. Abram became Abraham. Simon became Peter. Saul became Paul. The identity they discovered through an experience with God transformed them forever. Here are some examples of questions that might appeal to a person's identity in Christ:

- How are you different since you came to faith in Christ?
- Who are you now in Christ?
- Which character in the Bible most inspires you? What would he/she do in this situation? How can you emulate him/her?
- How would a child of the King respond to this problem?
- Because you have matured as a Christian, how will you handle this situation differently than you would have five years ago?

- *Resources of faith.* Coaches might remind people of available resources by asking a question such as, "Which of God's promises are available to help you meet this challenge?" When appropriate, coaches might share a reassuring verse, such as 2 Corinthian 9:8: *"And God is able to make every grace overflow to you, so that in every way, always having everything you need, you may excel in every good work."* Coaches might then ask a follow-up question:

  - How will God's grace enable you to meet this challenge?

- If God was willing to give His only Son to meet your biggest need, do you think He'll abandon you now?
- Currently, which of God's resources are you leaving on the table?

- *Calling.* When people clearly understand their divine calling, they rarely require external motivation. If they get sidetracked, a simple question can often re-orient them. The coach might ask, "How does achieving this goal fit into your calling? Or, "How would achieving this goal take you further down the path God has set before you?"

- *God-given passions and values.* I (Bob) desire efficiency in thought, action, and processes. God wired me that way. This coaching question would greatly motivate me: "What is the most efficient way for you to accomplish this goal?" Coaches should strive to understand the unique passions and values that influence people's behavior. Coaches can then build a mental bridge between clients' values and the actions they have committed to take.

- *Inherent strengths.* People who operate within their strengths tend to be more motivated than those who work outside their skill set. For example, young David declined Saul's armor and used a more familiar method to slay Goliath (1 Sam. 17). Who would have thought that a boy's slingshot could fell a giant! God often utilizes people's unique strengths to accomplish His purposes. For example, if God wired someone to lead, He may well draw upon those leadership skills when He gives them assignments. God does not waste gifts!

We would add one caution at this point. People tend to assume God will only call them to assignments that utilize their strengths. But numerous biblical examples suggest otherwise. Moses certainly did not feel confident as a public speaker, but God sent him to address Pharaoh. Gideon did not see himself as a natural leader, but God used him to rally his nation. Non-believers tend to trust their strengths. But Christians understand that God's strength is the key to success. God always equips people to complete their divine assignments.

Surprisingly, people are often unaware of their gifts. Someone may be a natural networker, yet merely assume she likes people. Or, a person may be a skilled problem solver, but worry he is simply meddling in other people's business. Coaches can guide people to develop a clear and accurate picture of their abilities.

A variety of resources are available to help people determine their strengths. The Bible contains several lists of spiritual gifts (Rom. 12; 1 Cor. 12; Eph. 4). Identifying how God has equipped them can prepare people to tackle their next challenge. Be aware, however, that people's spiritual gifting may shift over time. A spiritual gift is a divine equipping for a divine assignment. God may give someone a variety of assignments over the course of their life. As a result, the person's equipping may vary through the years. A good coach helps people recognize God's ongoing activity in their life.

Besides spiritual equipping, each person also has innate talents and character strengths. Here are some tools coaches might consider using to help clients identify innate strengths:

- *Strengths Finder* is an inventory intended to equip people to better employ their strengths and talents. This assessment is used in corporate settings to help employees excel in their strength areas, rather than achieving mediocre results in other fields. A companion book, *Living Your Strengths*, focuses on ways Christians can find and use their natural talents. Each book contains a code for an online inventory. Again, use this tool with caution. No inventory can capture or restrict who people are and how God can use them. Though knowing one's strengths is useful, God may choose to work through a person's weakness to demonstrate His power (2 Cor. 12:9).

- *Via Character Strengths* focuses on 24 character strengths that are most admired across cultures.[3] The free online inventory helps people identify their primary strengths. More in-depth reports are also available for purchase. Knowing a client's best character qualities enables the coach to

---

[3]To learn more about the Via Character Strengths survey, go to www.viacharacter.org

determine which line of questioning might spark the highest internal motivation. For example, if a person's character strengths include creativity and bravery, a coach might ask, "Which aspects of this task require bravery?" Or, "What is your most creative solution for this problem?"

- *Patterns of High Performance.* While developing an assessment to determine high performance types, Christian coach Dr. Jerry Fletcher discovered that each person succeeds at tasks and projects in a unique way. He developed a story-based process to help individuals identify when and how they work best. He outlines this procedure in his book *High Performance Patterns.*[1] Using this process, coaches can guide clients to understand how they operate most effectively.

- *Reward.* Some rewards are external, such as a job promotion or recognition. But rewards might also be internal. Coaches can draw on a person's internal reward system by asking questions like these: "How will you see yourself differently once you tackle this problem?" or "How will success change how you view future challenges?"

- *Awareness of Urgency.* People need to understand why they must take timely steps to achieve their desired outcome. Otherwise, they may resist action. In *Leading Change*, John Kotter states, "People

---

[1] Jerry L. Fletcher, *Patterns of High Performance* (Berrett-Koehler Publishers, 1993). To gain further training in the use of High Performance Patterns visit https://getpositive.today/get-positive-coach-training/.

will find a thousand ingenious ways to withhold cooperation from a process that they sincerely believe is unnecessary or wrong-headed."[5] He emphasizes that change leaders must help people understand why change needs to happen *now*. This principle also applies to coaches.

I (Bob) saw a sense of urgency take root in one pastor's soul as he faced a "now or never" deadline for a doctoral degree. I asked him why he needed to finish *now*. He responded, "Because I am losing credibility with my staff, my flock, and myself." He touched on one of his core values: setting a positive example for those he leads. As we worked to formulate a plan, we considered how much work remained, how long each segment would take to complete, and which activities he needed to remove from his weekly schedule to make time for his studies. I honestly doubted he could maintain the aggressive pace he set for himself. To my surprise, he did. He even achieved an award for his excellent work! He already possessed the passion he needed to accomplish his goal. I simply had the privilege of igniting it through a few thoughtful questions.

- *Desire to please God.* Christians long to hear the Lord say "well done, good and faithful servant" (Matt. 25:23). Coaches help people connect the dots between their goals and their personal

[5]John Kotter, *Leading Change* (Brighton Watertown, MA: Harvard Business School Press, 2012), 38. See also, John P. Kotter, *A Sense of Urgency* (Boston: Harvard Business Press, 2008).

relationship with God. When people sense their actions please God, their internal motivation soars. A coach might ask, for example, "What part of this accomplishment will most please the heart of God?" or "What must you do to hear God say 'well done, good and faithful servant' to you?"

CHOSEN ACCOUNTABILITY

People are far more likely to succeed when they set up their own accountability system. Here are some questions coaches may consider asking as they help clients develop a personalized system of accountability:

- What steps will you take to keep on track with your commitments?
- On a scale from 1 to 10, how committed are you to taking these steps?
- What do you need to do to stay on track?
- Who can you enlist to help you succeed?

Clients may want to enlist their coach as a part of their support team. While coaches may participate if they wish, they should strive to keep people answerable to God and responsible for themselves. Passivity becomes disobedience when people fail to complete the tasks God gives them.

A support system should encompass both strategies and people. These are a few accountability tactics coaches might recommend:

- Sharing commitments with loved ones and friends.

- Setting recurring cell phone reminders to prompt action.
- Strategically placed visual cues.
- Rituals, such as completing specific actions at certain times, places, or in conjunction with other habitual practices. For example, reading aloud a memory verse while going for a walk.
- Regular check-ins with an accountability partner.
- Appropriate personal rewards for achieving goals.
- Deliberately celebrating small wins along the way.
- Reflective journaling about successes and failures and the feelings and causes behind them.

For many people, accountability carries negative connotations. Perhaps it calls to mind a critical supervisor who detailed their every shortcoming or a father who was never satisfied with their performance. But coaches are encouragers, not overseers. When people fail, coaches help them learn from their mistakes so they fail forward.

Good coaches pay attention to verbal cues that suggest the client is avoiding personal responsibility. For example, if someone keeps saying "they," "he," and "her," rather than "I," "me," and "my," the person may have a skewed perspective. People might blame their spouse, children, boss, or colleagues for their shortcomings. They may explain that the economy has been bad, life has been too hectic, or their dog had to go to the vet. Of course, uncontrollable events occur from time to time. But wise coaches keep the focus on the client's actions. When the coachee starts blaming other people, the coach should gently but firmly redirect the conversation. The coach might use one of the following questions:

- That person is not in the room right now, so let's focus on you. What can you learn? What is within your control?
- What are you learning about yourself in this situation?
- What will you do differently moving forward to achieve success in this area?

Making excuses is often a learned response. Effective coaching guides people to accept personal responsibility. Some coaches take session notes with a special focus on commitments. In subsequent meetings, the coach may review the person's actions. The coach might say, for example, "In our last meeting you said you were going to take each of your adult children out for lunch. How did that go?" or, "You said you would join a local gym and begin exercising three mornings a week. How is that going?" While this practice involves an element of accountability, it also helps people track their progress. Coaches should ultimately measure success by people's accomplishments, not their words.

PRE-SESSION FORMS

Craig Faubel, a Blackaby-certified coach, works primarily with pastors and Christian business leaders. He developed a pre-session form that he has clients complete and send to him before each session. Their answers help him identify the session's focus. These are the questions he asks:

- What is God doing around me right now?
- What has He accomplished in and through me since our last meeting?
- What challenges am I facing that require prayer and/or His intervention?
- What opportunities has God opened up for me?
- Where am I currently hesitating to follow His leading?
- What does God want me to focus on with my coach, and what outcome does God want?
- To what goals and actions is God calling me to commit? By when?
- What does God want me to add to or subtract from my life to be more fully devoted to Him?
- What else is God placing on my heart?[6]

Accountability can radically strengthen one's resolve to undergo personal change and growth. For example, Bill can tell himself he needs to stop eating dessert until he loses ten pounds. But if no one else knows about his commitment, he might conveniently set it aside and indulge himself the next time his mother makes his favorite pie. If other people know about his goal, however, he is much more likely to experience success. Coaches should encourage their clients to develop a

---

[6]Used by permission. To learn more about the coaching services of Craig Faubel, or to contact him, go to www.blackabycoaching.org/coaches.

system of accountability that fits their personality type and lifestyle.

Coaches and clients should regularly review the effectiveness of the accountability systems they establish. With a good coach, even failure can be a springboard to success. On the other hand, if people persistently blame others and refuse any accountability, a leadership coach may not benefit them. In those cases, a coach can merely hold up a mirror so they clearly see what their inaction is costing themselves and others.

CONCLUSION

Chosen accountability is important because it enhances perseverance and sets the stage for future success. An accountability system works best when it taps into internal motivators. Futuring skills also help deepen and broaden insights and success. We'll discuss those next.

FOR REFLECTION AND DISCUSSION

1. What do you think of someone holding you accountable? What feelings does that produce?
2. When it comes to accountability, what difference does it make when people choose their own goals?
3. When does holding someone accountable become unhealthy?
4. Do you lean most naturally toward holding others accountable or empowering them to set up their own accountability system?

Futuring

Twelve Essential Coaching Skills

META-SKILLS

- Relationship-Building
- Awareness-Raising
- Focusing and Commitment
- **Futuring**

FUTURING META-SKILLS

Crystalizing a vivid, compelling vision of God's preferred future while anticipating and planning for challenges and embracing new insights.

FUTURING SKILLS INCLUDE:

10. Envisioning a God-Inspired Future (Chapter 15)
11. Anticipating and Overcoming Obstacles (Chapter 16)
12. Mining for Spiritual Takeaways (Chapter 17)

Envisioning a God-Inspired Future

I was in the Spirit on the Lord's day, and I heard a loud voice behind me like a trumpet saying, 'Write on a scroll what you see.'
John (Revelation 1:10-11)

So then, King Agrippa, I was not disobedient to the heavenly vision.
Paul (Acts 26:19)

A leader is someone who has a drive, commitment and most importantly, a vision and skill set to transform an idea into an innovation.
Daniel Transon

Reflecting on his first successful airplane flight, Orville Wright said, "I got more thrill out of flying before I had ever been in the air at all—while lying in bed thinking about how exciting it would be to fly!"[1] He dreamed of flying, and with work and determination, he eventually soared. Wright's vision propelled him to success at a time when most people believed flying was impossible. In fact, disbelief was so ubiquitous that no reporters came to witness the flights he and his brother Wilbur made day after day.[2]

Martin Luther King Jr. cast his vision of a more inclusive America on August 28, 1963, when he delivered this famous speech before 250,000 civil rights supporters:

> I have a dream that one day this nation will rise up and live out the true meaning of its creed: "We hold these truths to be self-evident; that all men are created equal."
> I have a dream that one day on the red hills of Georgia the sons of former slaves and the sons of former slave owners will be able to sit down together at the table of brotherhood.
> I have a dream that one day even the state of Mississippi, a state sweltering with the heat of injustice, sweltering with the heat of oppression, will be transformed into an oasis of freedom and justice.
> I have a dream that my four little children will one day live in a nation where they will not be judged

[1]Orville Wright, *How We Invented the Airplane: An Illustrated History* (Mineola, New York: Dover Publications, Inc., 2012), 78.
[2]David McCullough, *The Wright Brothers* (New York: Simon and Schuster, 2015), 116.

by the color of their skin but by the content of their character.

Wright's dream led him to fly. King's dream transformed a culture. Their experience speaks to the power and promise of vision.

Biblical vision differs from worldly vision, for it emanates not from people's imaginations but from God. Even the most selfish, diabolical fiend can imagine a future where he achieves his heinous desires. But that fantasy stems from his own selfish wishes. God is under no obligation to make people's dreams come true. Instead, He instills within the human soul a desire to accomplish His eternal purposes. Once people embrace God's call, their life proceeds with purpose and cohesion. People without vision lack direction. Their life merely becomes a series of opportunities, emergencies, and the empty pursuit of pleasure, which inevitably leads to despair and dissatisfaction. Likewise, ambitious visions birthed from people's imaginations—rather than God's revelation—lack God's blessing and heaven's resources.

According to A.W. Tozer, vision and leadership spring from earnest prayer: "Leadership requires vision, and whence will vision come except from hours spent in the presence of God in humble and fervent prayer?"[3] To know God's intentions, one must learn what is on His heart and mind (1 Sam. 2:35).

---

[3] A.W. Tozer and W. L. Seaver, *Prayer: Communing with God in Everything-Collected Insights from A. W. Tozer* (Chicago: Moody Publishers, 2016), 160.

Through insightful questions and observations, coaches can help people bring into focus a divine vision so rich and compelling they can almost taste, touch, and experience its wonder even before it comes to fruition. Once it takes firm root in a person's soul, a clear vision becomes a powerful motivator.

I (Bob) once coached a pastor who experienced a crisis of belief while struggling to complete his doctoral prospectus. He clearly lacked focus, a problem that stemmed from his low self-confidence. Despite his unquestionably successful ministry career, he viewed himself as an academic failure. His despair was negatively affecting his ability to lead his church. We determined together that he needed to finish his doctorate as a matter of stewardship. After removing some mental roadblocks, I asked him this refocusing question: "Tell me, how will you feel when you finally walk across that stage, the faculty stands in your honor, and the doctoral hood is placed on your shoulders?" This question planted a compelling mental image within him that grew stronger than all his disabling fears and propelled him to success.

How can coaches cultivate a heavenly vision within their clients? They should start by reviewing the ways God guided them in the past. If, for example, a pastor cannot recall a time when God led him to abort a divine assignment, he will be more likely to preservere in his present undertaking. Coaches might also help clients identify how God motivated them previously. Doing so might provide clues as to how God will bring about progress in their life in the future.

Once people identify what they need to accomplish, envisioning takes on an additional aspect—picturing God's preferred future. Coaches can begin the process by bringing the blessings of obedience into focus:

- Tell me, when all is said and done and you have achieved this goal, how will life be better for you? For your loved ones? In your work? For the kingdom?
- Who will be most pleased when God accomplishes this through you?
- What do you imagine God saying to you when you accomplish this? What will you say back to Him?
- How will you celebrate completing your goal?

As coaches listen, they should ask God to sharpen the vision within their client's soul. As clients perceive that God is initiating something in their life, the vision will take on a motivating *"this one thing I must do"* quality (Phi. 3:13).

Coaches should also consider biblical examples of how God inspired people. He promised to bring the Israelites to a land *"flowing with milk and honey"* (Ex. 3:8). God's words were rich with symbolism and easy to invision. Milk came from healthy cattle that grazed in lush pastures. God promised Moses a land characterized by peace and fertility. Honey was a sweet luxury. God told Moses the land would be *flowing* with God's goodness. Such images were powerfully motivating!

Coaches might ask people to describe the promise they sense God has given them for their organization. If the client is a church planter, the coach may ask him to describe his future church. Will it have a fancy coffee bar in the lobby surrounded by people excitedly visiting? Will the children's area be amazing? Will the church meet in a facility of its own or in the midst of a high-traffic community center? Better yet, what life changes will attendees experience? How will the realization of this vision fulfill kingdom purposes? Visions of future success can encourage church planters not to lose heart when they deal with innumerable challenges during the early stages of birthing a congregation.

A coach might ask a small business owner what her company will look like once it undergoes the significant changes she is implementing. Will the staff be highly motivated, unified, and creative? Will the company invest significant portions of its profits back into the kingdom of God? Will it make positive contributions to the local community? The coach might ask the owner for a virtual tour of her future company offices. Such exercises can be incredibly energizing. They can also be extremely insightful for coaches who are trying to understand people's goals.

One caution. Envisioning is not a name-it-and-claim-it exercise. In spiritual leadership coaching, coaches do not lead others simply to conjure up fantasies from their own imaginations or ambition. Instead, they cooperate with God in drawing out His vision for people. Just as adjusting the knob on binoculars brings vision into focus, coaches should use Spirit-led questions and observations to clarify what God has embedded within a person's soul. Spiritual envisioning is holy ground and should not be undertaken lightly. God does not promise to make everyone's dreams come true. But He is highly motivated to achieve His will in the world. When people align themselves with God's purposes, they gain access to all the wisdom, power, and resources of heaven. Ultimately, people do not serve a vision, but the living God who directs their steps and insures victory.

CONCLUSION

Even with God-initiated visions, clear goals, and specific commitments, unforeseen challenges can threaten to wash away the best-made plans. Great coaches help people prepare for the surprises that inevitably come.

FOR REFLECTION AND DISCUSSION

1. What is the first vision you received from God?
2. When have you chased your own dream? How did it turn out?
3. What is an area of your life or vision that needs to be brought into sharper focus so you can taste it, smell it, and hold it tightly through the storms ahead?
4. How has a vision God placed in your heart been inspiring you to make whatever sacrifice is necessary in order to eventually achieve it?

CHAPTER 16

Anticipating and Overcoming Obstacles

The best laid schemes of mice and men often go awry.
Robert Burns

*For which of you, wanting to build a tower, doesn't
first sit down and calculate the cost to see if he has
enough to complete it? Otherwise, after he has laid the
foundation and cannot finish it, all the onlookers will
begin to ridicule.*
Jesus (Luke 14:28-29)

*Many plans are in a person's heart, but the LORD's
decree will prevail.*
Proverbs 19:21

God intended for the Israelites to conquer Canaan and dwell in a land flowing with milk and honey. The Israelites were initially happy with the plan, but they soon ran into obstacles. Walled cities, hostile armies, and large Canaanite soldiers stalled the Israelites' progress. Overcome by fear, the disheartened Hebrews turned and fled back into the wilderness.

Such behavior, especially from God's people, is all too common. What went wrong? The Israelites had a God-inspired vision. They were motivated. They made progress. Then the wheels came off, and the rest is history.

Their problem—as is often the case—was their inability to persevere when they faced road blocks. An obstacle can be any person or circumstance that stands between people and God's will. Abraham's hurdle was a chronically barren wife. Joseph's was ten jealous older brothers. Nehemiah's was Sanballat, Tobiah, and Geshem. Elijah's was Ahab and Jezebel. David's was Goliath. The Rich Young Ruler's was money. Judas' was greed. Thomas' was doubt. Each person knew what he should do, but something stood in his way. Some managed to overcome challenges and eventually enjoy God's rewards. Others never did. As a result, they lived the remainder of their days in failure and regret, speculating about what might have been.

Countless organizations fail to take steps that would ultimately lead to success. Many strategies for church or corporate transformation are gathering dust in cabinets. Countless New Year's resolutions have fallen by the wayside. Why? Some of those plans were not prompted by God, so the initiatives never bore fruit. In other cases, God-inspired plans failed because unanticipated obstacles derailed them.

When people are prevented from moving forward with their plans, they often experience feelings of defeat, incompetence, and shame. They may quit trying or discard their original plan as untenable. Spiritual leadership coaches encourage people to persevere despite the obstacles. Challenges are inevitable; failure is not!

ANTICIPATING OBSTACLES

No one can foresee every potential pitfall. Enemies may rise up to thwart the plan. Finances might dry up. Trusted friends and colleagues sometimes fall short. Economic downturns, international crises, trade wars, national elections, terrorist attacks, scandals, and a plethora of other issues can stand between people and their goals. But by asking the right questions, coaches can empower their clients to become more resilient and better prepared when obstacles inevitably arise. Here are some questions coaches might ask:

- What might go wrong? What will you do if it does?
- What is the worst thing that could happen? What is the best thing that could occur?
- What is your Plan B?
- What variables are outside your control?
- What would a perfect storm look like for you right now? How are you prepared for it?
- Where are you currently vulnerable?

Coaches should help people think through possible responses to the "what ifs." They may need to encourage big picture people to explore details that might go wrong and possible responses if they do—the who, what, where, when, and how. On the other hand, coaches may need to help detail-oriented people remain calm despite their long to-do list. If, for example, a person believes God wants him to improve his health, these are some possibilities he and his coach might explore:

- *Physical* obstacles, such as encountering a rainy day when he plans to go for a jog.
- *Financial* barriers, such as when a gym membership costs more than he budgeted.
- *Emotional* challenges, including reluctance to wake up early in the morning to exercise.
- *Spiritual* hurdles, such as guilt over a recent failure.
- *Relational* difficulties, including friends and family who do not support his commitments.
- *Time constraints*, such as when he has to work late.

While people cannot know the future, they can prepare for it!

OVERCOMING OBSTACLES

Navigating challenges can be extremely unsettling. Coaches should take the following steps when assisting a distraught client.

First, the coach may need to help the person regain emotional control. The coach might say, "This appears serious, but not life-threatening. Should we take a quick inventory to see what important aspects of your life are still healthy and in order? Is God still on His throne? Does your family still love you? Have you managed to stay out of the cardiac ward?" While coaches should not minimize people's pain, most situations do not warrant hitting the panic button. While losing a key staff person or client is difficult, those problems are not as serious as a terminal illness or divorce. The first thing coaches might need to do, therefore, is work to calibrate the person's response to the problem.

Second, coaches should help people identify and quantify their problem. People often react to symptoms without recognizing the underlying cause. In the heat of the moment, people tend to over-generalize. For example, someone might say, "Since things have gone south in my company, all my best people are leaving me for my competitors." The coach could ask, "Which people are leaving?" The coach might follow up by asking, "How many of these people have actually resigned?" Perhaps only one person quit, but the client fears others will follow suit.

Coaches should also help the person assess the damage. The staff member who left the company might have been entrusted with significant responsibility. But he may have grown critical and disruptive. He might have created tense moments in otherwise harmonious staff meetings. Is his departure really so devastating? Sure, the company will have to replace him. But the end result might be better. Could this be a good time to reshuffle the entire executive staff? Some of them are ready for new challenges. Perhaps instead of merely filling a vacancy, the company could reorganize the staff so their roles better suit their passions. As the coach works through these issues, the client may realize that his devastating problem is actually a blessing in disguise.

Common wisdom purports that smoke signals a fire. True, but some burning items cause more smoke than others. Someone might enter a smoky house and assume the building is burning down. But after entering the kitchen, the person may discover a frying pan unattended on a burner. What first appeared to be a widespread blaze is actually a relatively self-contained, manageable flame. Likewise, when people make an appointment with a coach, they may feel panicked about the billowing smoke they find in their life and work. The coach can help them survey their situation to determine how much is merely smoke and how much is actually fire.

Third, coaches should help people consider the best ways to overcome obstacles. At this point, the coach might need to assure the person that most problems have a solution. We have seen people panic after receiving a hostile letter from an attorney. To the untrained eye, the threat of legal action seems to contain a lot of fire. The coach might encourage clients to refrain from any knee-jerk responses until they have evaluated the situation carefully and sought appropriate legal counsel. The key to success is to assume a viable response exists and then to search for it calmly.

Once someone has decided to seek the most prudent solution, a coach can help the person evaluate which approach best suits the situation. People might grow discouraged if the answer is not immediately apparent. Coaches may need to encourage their clients to persevere. They might ask, "How long did it take you to build this company? Are you going to let a five-minute phone call tear down something you took twenty years to build?" or "Your first attempts seem to have disappointed you, but all is not lost. Tell me again what make success important to you? Let's take a deep breath together and look at what you can still accomplish." At times, a coach's greatest contribution is helping someone see that defeat is not the only option!

CONCLUSION

Everyone experiences problems. Wise people anticipate and prepare for them. When issues arise, they remain composed and choose the best possible response. Then they stick with the plan, making minor adjustments as necessary. Spiritual leadership coaches can play a significant role in this process. In the next chapter, we will explore ways coaches can deepen the insights the client gains during each session by mining for takeaways.

FOR REFLECTION AND DISCUSSION

1. What tends to derail you when you are working on an important project?

2. Are your primary obstacles mental, emotional, spiritual, or physical?

3. What helps you most when you become distracted or discouraged?

4. What Bible verse most encourages you when you are unsure of your capabilities?

CHAPTER 17

Mining for Takeaways

*It is necessary ... for a man to go away by himself ... to
sit on a rock ... and ask,
'Who am I, where have I been, and where am I going?*
Carl Sandburg

*If the God of the universe speaks to you, you ought to
write it down.*
Henry Blackaby

People love telling and retelling their favorite stories.
These narratives are often beloved because they
describe vivid experiences that were funny, embarrassing,
or marked a turning point of some kind.

My (Richard) parents often recount the story of a
dramatic experience they had when I was a child. My
father was the pastor of a church in Southern California.
While attending a special service, my parents both
felt called to serve as international missionaries. At
the close of the meeting, they went to the altar and
dedicated themselves to go wherever God sent them.

The international mission board soon approved their application, and they were tentatively earmarked to relocate to Africa where my father would teach at a Bible college.

Then a crisis occurred. As a seven-year-old, I experienced several fainting spells. My parents took me to the doctor. He scheduled a battery of tests and concluded that I might have a brain tumor. He prescribed medication and monitored me carefully. The mission board suggested that moving to Africa would be unwise until my medical condition improved. My parents were disappointed. They had been certain God was preparing them to go.

A few weeks later, my father received a phone call he would never forget. A small, struggling congregation in Saskatoon, Canada, was in danger of disbanding unless the remaining members could enlist a pastor. They asked my father to take the job. My parents, having already prepared themselves to go anywhere God invited them, recognized that serving in this Canadian church was God's plan all along. They assumed missions meant traveling to a distant land. But my father grew up in Canada. He had prayed for revival in that nation for years. Now God was inviting him to minister in his native land.

Little financial support was available for my parents' ministry, so they relied on God's provision. He always supplied exactly what they needed at just the right time. On that difficult mission field, my parents learned that

God was not merely a doctrine to believe, but a personal God who wanted to walk with them daily.

In time, people began inviting my father to speak about walking with God and knowing His will. He eventually wrote a book about lessons he learned while serving in Canada. It was called *Experiencing God: Knowing and Doing the Will of God.*

The book deeply impacted a missionary who was serving in Asia. That missionary eventually became the president of the denomination's international mission organization. He asked my father to travel internationally and teach missionaries the truths he wrote about in the book. Throughout their ensuing ministry, my mother and father ministered in 115 nations.

In a conversation with the mission director one day, my father mentioned that my health had prevented our family from serving as missionaries in Africa many years earlier. The man insightfully told my father that he would have likely enjoyed a wonderful ministry in Africa, but he doubted he would have written *Experiencing God* if he had gone. And because he wrote that book, he ministered in not one but 115 nations. To date, *Experiencing God* has been translated into more than 40 languages and is widely used to equip believers around the globe.

When my parents surrendered to God's will, they set a number of divine initiatives into motion. Looking back over the milestone moments in their lives, they could clearly see how God guided them throughout their pilgrimage. They learned that, with God, a closed door may in fact open up an avenue for expanded service.

My parent's story has an interesting addendum. After moving to Canada, they connected me with doctors who could continue monitoring my brain tumor. The Canadian doctors ran the same tests the doctors in California had, but they found no trace of a tumor. They immediately discontinued the heavy medication I was taking, and I have never had another fainting spell.

Recognizing and remembering spiritual turning points is important. Sadly, many Christians fail to give these divine occasions the attention they deserve. A turning point for the Israelites was their exodus from slavery in Egypt. At the annual Passover meal, fathers would recount the exodus story to their families so they would never forget it. For New Testament Christians, communion and baptism are powerful reminders of dramatic spiritual turning points. Psalm 106 describes the disastrous consequences of forgetting God's past work (bolded for emphasis):

> *Both we and our fathers have sinned;*
> *we have done wrong and have acted wickedly.*
> *Our fathers in Egypt **did not grasp***
> ***the significance of your wondrous works***
> ***or remember your many acts of faithful love;***
> *instead, they rebelled by the sea—the Red Sea.*
> *Yet he saved them for his name's sake,*
> *to make his power known.*
> *He rebuked the Red Sea, and it dried up;*

he led them through the depths as through a desert.
He saved them from the power of the adversary;
he redeemed them from the power of the enemy.
Water covered their foes;
not one of them remained.
Then they believed his promises
and sang his praise.
They soon forgot his works
and would not wait for his counsel.
They were seized with craving in the wilderness
and tested God in the desert.
He gave them what they asked for,
but sent a wasting disease among them.
Psalm 106:6-15

Many people today do not like history. Perhaps they associate it with boring schoolteachers who droned on about meaningless dates and tedious events. Likewise, people often fail to look back on important turning points in their own life. But reflecting, especially on God's activity, is vitally important for Christians.

Spiritual attentiveness takes many forms. The following pages outline a number of ways coaches can help people practice personal and spiritual reflection.

SESSION TAKEAWAYS

During coaching sessions, God often reveals fresh insights about Himself and His purposes. The coachee can easily overlook these revelations. People tend to focus only on actions and outcomes, not on the spiritual lessons

God wants them to learn. For that reason, a Christian coach should help people mine their experiences for spiritual insights that may be just beyond their immediate awareness. A coach might ask one of these questions at the end of a session to provoke reflective thought:

- What stood out to you as we coached today?
- What have been your primary insights or takeaways during our time together?
- What do you sense God is saying to you?
- What difference will taking action on this insight make in your life? Your choices? Your relationships? Your work?
- What do you see or understand more clearly now?

Takeaway questions are powerful for two reasons. First, they leave people in charge of their own learning. Second, taking time each session to explore takeaways can help clients maintain a positive mindset during trying times.

As an alternative method of mining for session takeaways, coaches might consider giving the client a post-session reflection form. This method allows time, especially for introverted people, to reflect on the questions prior to responding.

LEARNING FROM SETBACKS AND FAILURES

Even with a coach's assistance, people fail from time to time. Good coaches help people mine the failure for takeaways so they do not end up in a similar situation again. These questions may help:

- This didn't turn out the way you/we had hoped. What can you learn from this?
- What went well? What did not work well?
- What will you do differently next time?
- What do you sense God saying to you right now?

JOURNALING

Writing in a journal is an excellent way to identify and document key life events. Not only do people benefit from slowing down and writing out their thoughts, but the journal can also become a record of God's activity and faithfulness in the person's life. Patterns of God's activity, commands, and promptings might emerge over time. These recurrences can alert people to ways God may use them in the future. One pattern I (Bob) noticed through reflective journaling is that God often calls me to minister in places of discouragement or disunity. While not an absolute indicator for me, patterns attract my attention as I seek the Lord's direction.

SYMBOLS

Performing a symbolic action, such as saving a keepsake from an important encounter with God, can serve as a useful reflecting tool. I (Richard) wrote a daily devotional book with my father, Henry, called *Experiencing God: Day by Day*. Many people have told us that God used a devotion from that book to direct them to a particular job. In response, they photocopied that page, framed it, and hung it on their office wall. When life becomes difficult—and it will—reminders of God's faithfulness and guidance in the past provide encouragement to hold the course.

SERMON INSIGHTS

Many pastors marvel when God speaks a word to congregants that only vaguely relates to their sermon. Preachers who worked hard to develop a particular message might find this phenomenon off-putting at first. But God speaks truth both through and alongside a pastor's homily. The apostle Paul referenced the paradoxical nature of preaching in 1 Corinthians 1:21: *"For since, in God's wisdom, the world did not know God through wisdom, God was pleased to save those who believe through the foolishness of what is preached."* The Holy Spirit applies the truth proclaimed through a sermon to the unique circumstances and heart of each listener.

After I (Richard) preach, people often tell me that God used something I said during my sermon to reveal a powerful insight to them. Interestingly, I often cannot remember saying what they claim to have heard. At times, I have even listened to a recording of the message and not found the statement they cited. I have come to understand that the Holy Spirit within people speaks to their heart while I preach. My declarations cannot change anyone, but one word from the Holy Spirit can transform a life. Whenever I preach, teach, or coach, I pray for the Holy Spirit to work in each listener's heart. Perhaps the 500 people in the congregation will hear

500 unique, divinely inspired messages (each of them better than the one I delivered!).

In coaching, spiritual insight may stem from a coach's perceptive question or timely comment. But God is not limited to working directly through spoken words and their intended meaning.

PROBING FOR OVERLOOKED INSIGHTS

Some people have never learned to recognize God's activity. He might be speaking loudly and clearly, but they do not recognize His voice. He may have accomplished a great work in their life, but they chalk it up to luck or happenstance. For example, a man who is concerned about his finances might pray for God's provision. Out of the blue, or so it seems, a friend from his college days contacts him and offers him a job. Many people, even Christians, would view this event as a coincidence. But an insightful coach might ask, "You have been praying for God to intervene in your finances. Then this happens, completely unrelated to anything you initiated. What might that mean? Could this be an answer to your prayer? Has God said 'yes'? How do you know if this is God's answer?" A spiritually perceptive person traces the workings of God's divine hand.

Coaches should actively look for "God moments" their clients may have missed. A client might say, "Then I happened to sit next to Jim at a restaurant." The coach could respond, "You *happened* to go to the same restaurant as the person who is able to help you with this problem?" Or the person might mention, "My wife really doesn't want me to take George on as a partner." The coach could respond, "You have been praying for God to warn you if this deal is not from Him, and now your wife has spoken against it. What a coincidence! What do you make of that?" While coaches should not place too much weight on insignificant events, they should be careful not to undervalue God's activity. His work is always worth taking seriously!

THE POWER OF FOCUS

Brain science speaks to the value of reflecting on life lessons. Harvard psychiatry professor John J. Ratey declares, "Our own free will may be the strongest force directing the development of our brains, and therefore our lives."[1] Daniel Goleman, pioneering author on the subject of emotional intelligence, writes, "Paying full attention seems to boost the mind's processing speed, strengthen synaptic connections, and expand or create neural networks for what we are practicing."[2] While people are often in a hurry to move on to the next problem at hand, coaches should encourage people to take time to fully process their latest insight.

Why should coaches help people fully embrace the insights they gain? Because when coaches lead someone to identify, value, and focus on a primary takeaway, they give the person the gift of focus. God is not passive in this process. He empowers people as they address the

---

[1] John J. Ratey, *A User's Guide to the Brain* (New York: Vintage Books, 2001), 17.
[2] Daniel Goleman, *Focus* (New York: HarperCollins Publishers, 2015), 164.

priorities He presses into their awareness. God expects people to "set their minds" on the right issues. Notice how that phrase shows up in Scripture:

> "Now determine in your mind and heart to seek the LORD your God" (1 Chron. 22:19).
>
> "For those who live according to the flesh have their minds set on the things of the flesh, but those who live according to the Spirit have their minds set on the things of the Spirit. Now the mind-set of the flesh is death, but the mind-set of the Spirit is life and peace" (Rom. 8:5-6).
>
> "Set your minds on things above, not on earthly things" (Col. 3:2).

Many people struggle to "set" their mind. In an age of multitasking, people are unaccustomed to thinking deeply about one issue. Yet many of the problems people face today can only be resolved through prolonged, analytical, God-inspired thought. Such thinking is not haphazard or casual. God designed the human mind to accomplish great feats. But people must first train and focus it. Coaches can teach people to think in a more disciplined and perceptive manner.

People can find some of the greatest reservoirs of personal insight in their failures. By keeping an optimistic outlook, coaches can turn people's shortcomings into opportunities for spiritual growth. If someone crumbled under the pressure of a problem, coaches can help mine the experience for takeaways so the person does not repeat the mistake. The coach might ask one of these questions:

- What might you learn from this?
- What are your takeaways?
- Where do you believe God wants you to go from here?

With God, there is always another chapter to the story!

CONCLUSION

When coaches mine the coaching conversation for spiritual takeaways, they empower people to align their life with what is truly important. In the next chapter, we will examine coaching in real time and under specific and sometimes vexing circumstances.

FOR REFLECTION AND DISCUSSION

1. What does the biblical phrase *"set your mind"* (Col. 3:2) mean to you?
2. How well do you keep track of the insights God gives you?
3. Do you keep a journal? If not, purchase one and begin recording what God is saying and doing in your life. Be sensitive to record any sense of direction or guidance God gives you.
4. When have you initially missed an important takeaway from an experience with God? Why did you not recognize what God was doing? How have you improved over time at identifying God's hand in your life?

Putting it All to Work

CHAPTER 18

Coaching through Seasons of Pain

By Brett Pyle

Note: Brett is an extraordinarily gifted coach who has helped countless executives overcome personal and professional hurdles to achieve great results. In this chapter, Brett presents a model that can be a helpful coaching tool. However, Brett is also highly responsive to the Holy Spirit's leading throughout his coaching sessions and makes adjustments when necessary.

God whispers to us in our pleasures, speaks to us in our conscience, but shouts in our pains; pain is His megaphone to rouse a deaf world.
C.S. Lewis

If you only respond to God and yield to Him in times of pain, He certainly knows what number to dial to reach you!
Richard Blackaby

Roger (name has been changed) grew up on the tough streets of the Bronx. He was strong, talented, and charismatic. Everyone liked him. Many opportunities came his way, not all of them wholesome. He enjoyed a fast, hard-partying lifestyle. Shortly before he turned eighteen, however, the good times ended abruptly. Intoxicated, Roger drove over a hill and crashed directly into a parked car, critically injuring its occupant. Roger could not remember the event when he awoke in the hospital. Barely an adult, Roger found himself in prison for nearly a year.

Jail made Roger hard and angry. Shortly after his release, he sat miserably on his front porch steps and glared at passersby. He seethed with anger that a single stupid mistake had ruined his life. He left the steps and took a long walk. Along the way, he had a tough conversation with himself. He concluded that he alone was to blame for his circumstances. By the time he returned home, he had accepted personal responsibility for his situation and vowed to fix his own mess. No more pity party.

Fast forward 25 years.

Roger succeeded where many fail. He worked menial day jobs to pay his way through night school, eventually earning a degree in accounting and finance. He landed a job in the accounting department of a sizeable company and worked his way up the ranks. He met and married the girl of his dreams. Ultimately, a huge new career opportunity came his way. He was offered a position as the CFO of a rapidly growing company. He took the job and quickly made a name for himself. He worked long hours and saved the owners millions of dollars. As a result, they appointed him CEO and gave him partial ownership of the company. His life appeared to be back on track.

I began coaching Roger when he was near the precipice of his career. On the surface, everything was going his way. He told me he did not have any "real problems." He simply wanted to sharpen his leadership abilities. But deep pain often lurks below the surface of seemingly successful lives, as Roger would soon discover.

PAIN'S POSSIBILITIES

Personally, I am not highly motivated to help people improve incrementally. I find more satisfaction in equipping clients to undergo significant life change. And in my experience, breakthrough life transformation rarely occurs while everything is going well. Just as a caterpillar's struggle against the resisting walls of its chrysalis strengthens and fortifies its wings, pain typically precedes the birth of a newly formed attribute in a person's life.

Spiritual leadership coaches are invaluable in the transformation process. They are objective, for they are not experiencing their client's pain. Instead, they walk with the person through the pain, much like a midwife assists a laboring mother. They can also help people recognize God's purposes in difficult life seasons. To paraphrase C.S. Lewis, God has people's undivided attention in their discomfort. He uses it to purify and transform them. In a way, a client's pain can be a coach's ally. Wise coaches use it to move people from where they are to where God wants them to be.

How do skilled coaches find pain? Sometimes it is immediately obvious. On other occasions, the coach must dig to find it. The Spiritual Pain Funnel, which I adapted and modified from a marketplace model, can help coaches locate pain.[1]

THE SPIRITUAL PAIN FUNNEL

The Spiritual Pain Funnel

Surface Issues

Minor Annoyances

Problems Requiring Attention

Reasons for Changing

Personal Impact of Not Changing

Clear Spiritual Calling for Change

Crisis of Belief /
Decision Time!

---

[1] A similar model, presented during a Sandler Sales Training class that I took years ago, inspired this adapted illustration. For more on the Sandler Sales model, go to: https://www.sandler.com/blog/asking-questions.

Using the Spiritual Pain Funnel as a guide, coaches can ask clients a series of progressive questions that move them from merely accepting the *status quo* to experiencing major life transformation.

At the beginning of the conversation, clients may not acknowledge a particular problem they wish to address. Roger maintained the *status quo* in the opening story of this chapter, claiming he had no need to make major changes. He simply wanted to improve his leadership skills. For illustrative purposes, picture the *status quo* hovering above the oft-murky waters of the Spiritual Pain Funnel.

A simple question (e.g., "What's going on?") can identify *surface issues* in someone's life. These issues might initially appear insignificant. Clients may not even consider them important enough to address with a coach.

A follow-up question (e.g., "Really?") might encourage further explanation, revealing *minor annoyances*. Again, the person might think these irritations are "not a big deal." But they offer the coach a glimpse of what lies below the surface. Expressing understanding or empathy can progress the coach deeper into the funnel. A mere "I see," or "oh," followed by silence often reassures the person that the coach is sympathetic, listening, and interested in hearing more.

As the client continues to speak, spiritual leadership coaches should practice multi-level listening skills and take note of deeper concerns, specifically issues that could lead to serious consequences if left unaddressed. For example, the coach might pick up on a non-verbal reaction or nuanced shift in tone when the coachee mentions a particular annoyance. In a long-term coaching relationship, the coach might notice when a client references an annoyance that is similar to a problem they mentioned in past sessions. Alternatively, the coach might simply ask, "Which of those annoyances is troubling you most at the moment?" This question encourages the coachee to reflect more deeply on the list of disturbances.

Once clients zero in on a particular problem, coaches may feel as though they have already succeeded. After all, "the problem named is half solved." Right? Yes and no. Everyone's pain tolerance is different. A discomfort that spurs one person to action could simply be everyday life for someone else. Purposeful queries can help clients articulate *specific reasons change is necessary now*. The following questions can help people brainstorm reasons for changing:

- How long has this been going on?
- What might happen if you let this situation go unchecked?
- Where else in your life is this problem an issue?
- Why is this such a big deal?

Though offering vague justifications for changing is a good start, people must personalize these reasons in order to reach the next level in the funnel. Why? Because pain that leads to change is almost always personal. The problem does not merely affect the person's organization. It carries personal consequences. The following questions can help people feel and articulate *the personal impact of not changing*:

- What is this issue costing you personally (Note: costs often show up in more than one arena—money, time, stress, peace of mind, reputation.)?
- How does allowing this situation to persist reflect on you as a leader (Or any number of other roles: spouse, parent, pastor, manager, Christian, provider, steward, employee, teacher, etc.)?
- If nothing changes, what will happen five years down the road?
- How might this issue impact your legacy?

Merely acknowledging pain is not enough. People must take specific steps to address it. Once someone quantifies the personal impact of not changing, coaches may need to offer a final challenge. Questions like these might be appropriate:

- What are you prepared to do about this problem?
- How much longer are you willing to put up with this?
- There's clearly a lot at stake for you, but I'm thinking you're not prepared to take action. How am I wrong?
- If it were all this simple, I'm thinking you would have done something long ago. Why now?

- You've tried to address this issue before. What is different this time?
- Are you sure you want to move forward? "No" is an okay answer (This is one of the few situations where a yes or no question is appropriate. As that wise sage Yoda once mused: "Do or do not. There is no try!")!

The all-important final stage in the Spiritual Pain Funnel moves the coachee from knowing the *personal impact of not changing* to making a *clearly stated commitment to change*. It is effectively "calling the question." Is the person ready to make a commitment? The decision is up to the coachee. It *always* is in the coaching relationship.

This moment in the coaching session is crucial. In an openly spiritual setting, the coach might invite the client into a time of prayer. I have never had anyone decline such an invitation. I usually begin the prayer with a question:

"Lord, You've been present here in our conversation. What do You want [person's name] to hear from You right now? Are You calling him/her into action? If so, to what action are You calling him/her? We'll just wait here silently in Your presence for You to speak."

After praying, I remain silent until the client reacts, twitches, speaks, or otherwise indicates the Spirit has moved. The only follow up questions I ever ask are these:

- What did you hear?
- What are you going to do now?

Sometimes the person hears nothing during the initial prayer time, so we return to a time of silent waiting. As we seek God a second time, the coachee often encounters Him powerfully. Afterward, I repeat my questions:

- What did you hear?
- What are you going to do now?

I give the person time to respond and then we typically end the session by praying for strength and obedience to persevere through the crisis of belief that will inevitably follow the person's decision to align with God's agenda.

People might progress through the Spiritual Pain Funnel during multiple coaching sessions spanning several months, or they might complete the process during a single encounter. The principles are the same even if the client does not have a saving relationship with Christ.

Let's revisit our friend Roger—who is not a believer—to illustrate how this process played out in his life.

THE SPIRITUAL PAIN FUNNEL – IN PRACTICE

Uncovering deep pain in Roger's life took about eight months of coaching. During an early session, we processed an issue involving an underperforming key executive on his team. Dan (name has been changed) had been a high achiever, but his role had seemingly outgrown his capabilities.

"It's not a big deal, but I'll have to let him go," Roger said. He planned to hire a replacement, but he would handle the role himself in the meantime. He had filled in for people before. So Roger fired Dan. The company paid Dan severance. Roger's workload increased as he personally assumed management of Dan's former team.

Several months later, we discussed a significant issue Roger's wife (we'll call her Susan) had. She had become dependent on prescription pain medications and was not fulfilling her responsibilities as a mother, homemaker, and wife. She and Roger put together a plan of action. They enlisted professional therapists and counselors. Everything was back on track, although Roger's responsibilities at home increased.

Three or four months later, a new problem emerged. Roger told me the story at a restaurant over dinner. While his company was doing great, another previously high-performing direct report (we'll call him Andrew) was falling apart. Roger had hired him many years earlier and promoted him through the ranks. But now his "head just wasn't in the game." As Roger discussed Andrew's ineffectiveness at length, his tone and tenor became increasingly agitated. Perhaps Andrew's divorce was impacting his performance, Roger said. Maybe something else was causing it. But the guy would have to go.

"Wait a minute, Roger. I'm confused," I said. "Are we talking about Andrew or Dan?"

Roger responded to my feigned confusion with anger. "What do you mean? Can't you keep up with the story? We're talking about Andrew. Dan's been gone for months," Roger said. "I thought you were supposed to be a good coach. Perhaps I need to find a new one."

"Oh! We're talking about me now," I replied. "That's good, because for a moment I thought we were discussing Susan again."

A heavy silence hung in the air as the implications of my words sunk into Roger's mind. He thought through each of his troubled relationships, eventually recognizing the common denominator: himself. He was visibly shaken. After several minutes, Roger returned his focus to me.

"You just blew my mind," he blurted out, his eyes welling with tears.

I returned his gaze, my own eyes watery, and mouthed a single word: Sorry. Then we sat in silence.

"So, what's going on in you right now?" I asked after several minutes.

"I feel like I'm on the verge of seeing something clearly, but I can't quite make it out," Roger said.

"Want some help?" I asked.

"Yes. That's why you're here!"

"You may not like it. Are you sure you want me to continue?"

Roger's direct, bring-it-on gaze spoke louder than his words as he told me he was ready to hear my assessment.

"Ok. Here's what I see," I told him. "I see a man who has accomplished a great deal. More than most. You've emerged from difficult circumstances, and you've succeeded by taking responsibility for your problems. Now I see you challenging others to own their shortcomings as well."

Roger nodded affirmatively, urging me to go on.

"When people don't meet your demanding expectations, *they* become the problem," I continued. "You become increasingly demanding, causing them more stress and lowering their performance further. The cycle continues until you eventually let them go. Each time you do, it costs you: broken relationships, stress, severance, and an increased workload, because no one can do the job as well as you."

From Roger's slight wince, I knew the last phrase hit close to home.

"I'm sure I'm probably off on some of this," I said. "So you tell me. What's the real problem here, Roger?" I asked.

"I think my perfectionistic tendencies are stifling everyone around me," Roger quickly responded. "I want to bring out the best in them, but instead they cave under the pressure I put on them."

"Well said," I replied. "Who's the problem then?"

"I guess I am," Roger said without conviction.

"Of course, we know that's 'the right answer,'" I said, sensing I needed to challenge Roger to make the case for himself. "All we can ever control is ourselves and our actions. But, so what! You demand a lot from people. The best bosses always do. What's the big deal? It's worked well for you so far. Why change now?"

A long silence followed, during which Roger clearly reflected on his life circumstances, the reasons he needed to change, and the toll his behavior was taking on his relationships. I let the silence hang in the air for a while, then I pushed harder to help him see the *personal impact of not changing.*

"This issue with Susan," I said. "We're not talking severance here. What's this one going to cost you?"

"Half of everything I own. Perhaps more. Maybe my relationship with my son." Roger choked out that final sentence. Then the breakdown came. He released the tears he had held back for many years.

I sat with him in silence for several minutes.

"That's a tall price to pay," I finally said as he regained his composure.

He nodded in agreement.

"What would it look like if you returned from our little 'walk off your front porch steps' completely owning this situation like you did so many years ago?" I asked.

"I think I'm there now. I know I'm the problem, and I know I must change," Roger said firmly.

"Wow. Coming from you, that's a powerful statement. How about we start there next time?"

Roger agreed, and we both knew we had covered a lot of ground that evening.

As we left the restaurant, Roger gave me an uncharacteristic bear hug. "You never described that crap in the coaching brochure," he said.

"No, I guess I didn't. Sorry about that."

For the first eight months of our coaching relationship, Roger and I stayed in the top half of the pain funnel. He expressed his *status quo* (everything is fine), some *surface issues* and *minor annoyances* (underperforming employees), and even a few *problems requiring attention* (Susan's chemical dependency). We coached around those issues, and I helped Roger make incrementally better decisions in each situation.

Then, during a single evening, we broke into the lower half of the funnel and opened the door for Roger's transformation as a leader. He came face to face with the core problem he needed to address. He stated the reasons he needed to make adjustments and the personal cost if he didn't. He left the session knowing he needed to change. The productivity of our future coaching sessions grew exponentially after that encounter.

The path to transformation is the same for both Christians and unbelievers: *"Be transformed by the renewing of your mind"* (Rom. 12:2b). Spiritual leadership coaches have the noble privilege of joining God's activity in people's lives.

Of course, coaches must create a safe environment so clients feel comfortable opening up to them. Many coaches fail at this task and thereby miss the opportunity to join God in His transformative work. Creating an environment of trust takes time. In Roger's case, we spent eight months of foundational trust-building work before he experienced a breakthrough.

But I would like to conclude this chapter by making the case that painful seasons can expedite the process. Using a tool called *vulnerability*, the coach and coachee can establish the appropriate level of trust in a single conversation.

Vulnerability opens people up as quickly as superiority shuts them down. As I type, I am flying home from a speaking engagement. I spent two hours teaching a group of senior-level business executives how to live a life of significance and purpose. In my talk, I used an example of a personal failing I experienced when I parented my son for perfection, a pressure I felt in my childhood home. The story casts me in an unflattering light. I've told it hundreds of times, but it affects me every time. It impacts the audience too. I can tell because I often notice their eyes moisten as they listen. As a result, they connect to *their* story.

Before I left the workshop, a participant approached me. "You don't know me from Adam, but the story you shared really moved me," he said. "The same thing is happening to me with my kids, and I also sense it stems from the way I was parented."

He then broke down and confessed that he was trapped in a cycle of parenting for perfection, despite vowing he would never be like his father. In that moment of brokenness, the man became openly coachable.

We quickly journeyed down the pain funnel. Hearing my story of failure prompted him to address his own shortcomings. He clearly saw the reason to change, and he understood the multi-generational impact of *not* changing.

"Do you want to be free?" I asked.

"Yes, I do," he responded through sobs.

I allowed the silence to hang in the air for a few moments. "Ok. Let's get to work."

Jesus once greeted a lame man at the pool of Bethesda with a question similar to the one I asked the hurting father (John 5:1-15). After the lame man had spent 38 years laying by the side of the pool, Jesus asked, "Do you want to be well?" Some say a more complete and accurate translation of this question would be, "Do you want to be all you were created to be?" The honest answer to this question becomes apparent when people are deeply in touch with their own pain. A superficial "yes" does not lead to transformation. A deeply felt response coupled with commitment does.

PROGRESSING DOWN THE PAIN FUNNEL

If you have	Ask these kinds of questions ...	To uncover
Status Quo	What's going on? What's happening right now? What's the current state of your life? ... your family? ... your organization? ... your church? ...your leadership team? Where do you want it to be?	Surface Issues

Surface Issues	Tell me more. And? What else? What's not working? But that's probably not a source of irritation?	Minor Annoyances
Minor Annoyances	Why is that keeping you up at night? Why is that such a big deal? But that's probably not all that important? So what?	Problems Requiring Attention
Problems Requiring Attention	So what? How long has that been a problem? What have you tried so far? How did that work? If nothing changes, what would happen?	Reasons for Changing
Reasons for Changing	How much has that cost you? How does that impact you personally? What is your _____ (spouse, child, parent, co-worker) saying to you about that? What does that say about you? Your leadership ability? How do you feel about that? What if it never changes? And...? What's the impact on you if you don't make a change in this area? And? What else?	Personal Impact of Not Changing

Personal Impact of Not Changing	Have you given up trying to deal with it? What do you sense God is doing here? ...is saying to you? ...wants you to do? How do you know that? Circumstances? Scripture? Prayer? Counsel of other believers? But you're probably not sure about that? Let's take some time to pray right now. What's God calling you to do?	Clear Spiritual Calling for Change
Clear Spiritual Calling for Change	How committed are you to change in this area? Really? What are you prepared to do? What's next?	Decision to Change

CONCLUSION

When coaches join God's work in someone's life, they often enter that person's pain. Prayer should be a close companion during these seasons. Pain either drives people into God's arms or embitters them toward Him. Spiritual leadership coaches should be prayer warriors on behalf of their clients.

A frequent source of pain is change, which often catches people by surprise. Coaches can help their clients address that pain by empowering them to navigate the shifting seasons of their lives. We will look next at how to effectively navigate life's changing seasons.

FOR REFLECTION AND DISCUSSION

1. What role has pain played in molding your character?
2. Which has shaped you more: pain or positive experiences?
3. What area(s) of pain in your life have you not yet addressed?
4. What cautions should you consider when coaching people through pain?
5. How might you become more effective in helping people process their pain?

CHAPTER 19

Coaching People through the Seasons of Life

Live each season as it passes; breathe the air, drink the drink, taste the fruit, and resign yourself to the influences of each.
Henry David Thoreau

May you live all the days of your life.
Jonathan Swift

1 To everything there is a season, A time for every purpose under heaven:
2 A time to be born, And a time to die; A time to plant, And a time to pluck what is planted; 3 A time to kill, And a time to heal; A time to break down, And a time to build up; 4 A time to weep, And a time to laugh; A time to mourn, And a time to dance;

5 A time to cast away stones, And a time to gather stones; A time to embrace, And a time to refrain from embracing; 6 A time to gain, And a time to lose; A time to keep, And a time to throw away; 7 A time to tear, And a time to sew; A time to keep silence, And a time to speak;

8 A time to love, And a time to hate; A time of war, And a time of peace.

9 What profit has the worker from that in which he labors? 10 I have seen the God-given task with which the sons of men are to be occupied. 11 He has made everything beautiful in its time. Also He has put eternity in their hearts, except that no one can find out the work that God does from beginning to end.

Ecclesiastes 3:1-11

I (Richard) was the president of a seminary in Canada for 13 years. The school was located in Cochrane, Alberta, a bustling town in the foothills of the majestic Rocky Mountains. My family loved living in that area. I had a great leadership team. My career blossomed. I assumed I would remain in that comfortable, fulfilling role until I retired.

But my life slowly began to change. I started receiving job offers from various Christian organizations. I declined the invitations, but they made me wonder if I was open to a major life change.

Then God used a Christian friend to challenge me. He said he had been praying for me, and he sensed I needed to leave the seminary and work full-time with my father's ministry. I had written and spoken with my father regularly over the years, but I had never considered quitting my "day job" to join his small organization. He was 71. Abandoning my stable position at the seminary to work with him didn't seem like a great career move!

Nevertheless, that conversation with my godly friend set into motion monumental life changes. I was already scheduled to speak with my father in St. Louis the following day. While we were together, I told him about my recent conversation and asked him what he thought. He said he needed to consult my mother.

The next morning, my dad gave me his answer. "I talked with your mother," he said. "We both agree that having you become the president of our ministry would be an answer to our prayers!"

I made the transition several months later.

Within days of starting my new job with Blackaby Ministries International (blackaby.org), my father experienced his first major health setback. We didn't know it at the time, but winter was gradually setting in on my father's illustrious ministry. He needed someone to assist him. I needed a change as well. I loved my job at the seminary, but I had stopped growing. Though I regularly faced obstacles, they were usually similar to problems I'd tackled many times before. I needed to move on to new challenges and make room for the next leader God had prepared for the school.

At the time, I understood little about life's seasons. Since then, I have realized that my father and I were both experiencing winter, and we were unknowingly preparing to enter a glorious new spring.

Though inevitable, change frequently catches people off guard and causes enormous stress. The writer of Ecclesiastes made some powerful statements about dealing with life's transitions (Ecc. 3:1-11).

LIFE FLOWS IN SEASONS.

Scripture declares that everything in life has a season.[1] Though the climate differs in various regions around the globe, many places experience four distinct seasons annually: spring, summer, fall, and winter. *Spring* is the season for planting. *Summer* is a time of growth and maturity. What was planted in spring ripens under the heat of the summer sun. *Fall* is the season to harvest what was planted in spring and matured in summer. Finally, *winter* is a time of endings. In God's economy, however, a new spring always follows on the heels of winter.

While this cycle is easy to recognize in nature or farming, most people have never learned that their life follows this pattern. For example, a person might land a great new job and enter a *spring* in his career. He has plenty to learn, and he is unsure if he can master the necessary skills. He wonders if he will get along with his colleagues or survive the probationary period. But spring

---

[1]For an extensive treatment of this subject, see Richard Blackaby, *The Seasons of God: How the Shifting Patterns of Your Life Reveal His Purposes for You.* (Colorado Springs: Multnomah/Waterbrook Publishers, 2012).

holds great potential too. Even though he is nervous, he is excited about where this new position could lead. He soon enters *summer*, a time of hard work and growth. He masters his responsibilities and becomes a skilled employee. In time, he is promoted to management. He has entered *fall*. Rather than learning his job, he teaches others how to master theirs. He enjoys the rewards of working hard in summer. But *winter* ultimately comes. His job no longer challenges him. He fears he is growing stale and complacent. One day, the leading company in his field offers him a management position. He accepts the job, and his team throws a farewell party. He packs his bag and leaves the familiar office building for the last time. On Monday, he joins the new company and starts learning the ropes. *Spring* begins again.

Understanding life's seasons can help coaches as they work with clients who are undergoing transitions. Perhaps someone is entering a new spring and feels overwhelmed by the complexities of her new role. Or maybe the person is toiling in the heat of a summer season and needs encouragement to stay the course. A client may have entered a fall season and finally experienced success. Or perhaps the coachee is entering winter. These transitions can be unsettling, troubling, and exhilarating. When placed within the context of God-designed seasons of life, however, they are manageable. Seasons add flavor and excitement to an otherwise mundane, predictable existence.

EVERYTHING IN LIFE HAS A PROPER TIME.

The difference between highly successful people and those who experience failure is often not skills or knowledge, but timing. To live a fulfilling life, people must do the right thing at the right time.

The writer of Ecclesiastes offers several meaningful examples of divine timing. The author states that there is *a time to be born and a time to die* (3:2). One of those options is far more attractive than the other! But Scripture teaches that each of these events plays an important role in a meaningful life. When people endure a painful ending, they may assume they made a mistake or God is punishing them. In truth, they might simply be experiencing the full gamut of an abundant, seasonal life.

Healthy lives do not merely include beginnings. Knowing when to embrace an ending is equally important. People often allow seasons to remain in their life past their expiry date. They stay at a job too long, cling to a friendship even after it has grown unhealthy, or hold on to practices that have become ineffective. Wise people know when to let something die a natural death.

Scripture indicates that there is *a time to plant and a time to pluck* (3:3). Again, people are typically more attracted to plucking than planting. After all, they can immediately eat what they pluck, but they must wait to enjoy what they plant. Impatient people are often tempted to rush the process. They begin a job, embrace a new habit, or enter a relationship and immediately look for a harvest. But when people are in a season of planting, they should not expect to be plucking! Coaches can be helpful in this process. If someone complains about a lack of results the coach might ask, "What season are you in? Is this a time of plucking or planting?" Perhaps the person should focus on planting seeds that will produce a future harvest.

Scripture states that there is *a time to build up and a time to break down* (3:3). Leaders often focus on the former and neglect the latter. Consider the following scenario. A pastor arrives at a new church and discovers that the evening service has been poorly attended for years. The congregants ask him to breathe new life into it. So he rolls up his sleeves and tries to save the service. He works hard on his sermons, urges people to attend, and even organizes an ice cream fellowship for after the meeting. Nonetheless, only a modest group of faithful diehards attends. The pastor becomes frustrated by his inability to draw a crowd. His coach might ask, "Is this a time to build up or dismantle the evening service? Has it served its purpose? Is there something new God wants you to do instead?" Viewing leadership responsibilities from a seasonal perspective sheds new light on difficult issues.

Ecclesiastes teaches that there is *a time to embrace and a time to refrain from embracing* (3:5). This principle applies to any relationship. Leaders tend to believe a larger staff is better and that filling a vacancy is more desirable than leaving it empty. When a viable candidate applies for the job, they may feel inclined to "embrace" the person. But the applicant might not be the person God has prepared for the position. One of my (Richard) errors as a leader was hiring "the best available" person. I would examine resumes and choose the most qualified candidate. But my method was flawed. Sometimes the right person had not yet applied for the job. I discovered that leaving a position vacant is better than hiring the wrong person.

As coaches help clients make difficult personnel decisions, they might ask, "How excited are you about this person joining your team?" Or, "How do the other team members feel about this person? Any red flags?" My (Richard) wife has an uncanny ability to discern who would make a good employee. Hiring someone she had not approved always turned out to be a mistake. Perhaps I needed a coach to ask, "How does your wife feel about this person?"

At other times, people refrain from hiring a candidate, enlisting a coach, or initiating a friendship even after God clearly tells them to move forward in the relationship. People squander opportunities when they act sluggishly. The key is knowing when to embrace.

Finally, Ecclesiastes teaches that there is *a time to speak and a time to remain silent* (3:7). Before talking, people should ask themselves, as Robert Greenleaf suggested, "In saying what I have in mind will I really improve on the silence?"[2]

---

[2]Robert K. Greenfield, *Servant Leadership* (New York: Paulist Press, 1977), 17.

I (Richard) once spoke to a mother who was frustrated that her young adult son would not speak to her about anything substantive in his life.

"How can I get him to talk to me about his life?" she asked.

"Who says he needs to talk with you?" I responded.

She looked shocked. "Because I am his mother and I am very concerned about him," she replied.

"Very well," I said. "But who says you should be the one to guide him through those issues?"

The mother was understandably concerned about her son and wanted to help him. But she had not considered that her well-intended advice might not be the most effective method of assisting him. Rather than continuing to offer unsolicited advice, the woman began listening to her son and to God's guidance.

This section of Ecclesiastes concludes by declaring everything is beautiful *in its time* (3:11). God's plan is perfect. But when people take matters into their own hands, life gets messy. For example, having a baby is wonderful. But having a baby as an unwed seventeen-year-old inevitably leads to problems and disappointments. Leaving a management position to start a new business can be exhilarating. But doing so without having adequate startup capital often leads to sleepless nights. Coaches can help people determine whether they are moving forward in their own timing or God's. In the following pages, we have included examples of questions coaches might ask clients depending on which season they are currently experiencing.

QUESTIONS FOR SPRINGTIME—NEW BEGINNINGS

- What most excites you about this opportunity?
- What do you sense God is saying or doing as you begin this new venture?
- How will you have to grow to succeed in this new endeavor?
- What will success require? What else?
- What are the major challenges for you in this new position? How will you manage your feelings of inadequacy?

QUESTIONS FOR SUMMER—HARD WORK

- What do you need to adjust or suspend temporarily so you can finish this job?
- How much time will this project take? Where will you fit it into your schedule?
- How will you protect your relationships during this busy season?
- Who can you enlist to help? Who else?
- What promises or resources from God are available to you right now?
- How can you avoid growing weary in well doing (Gal. 6:9)?
- How are you maintaining your strength, health, and enthusiasm during this demanding time?

- What outcome will make this season of hard work most worth your effort? What would encourage you to finish well?

QUESTIONS FOR AUTUMN—HARVESTING

- How has God's faithfulness been evident in these results?
- What else do you need to learn and/or celebrate?
- Who do you need to thank for this outcome? Who else?
- How does this harvest connect to the overall purpose or vision of this company/church/organization?
- As you enjoy this season of harvest, who can you personally mentor so they can one day reap a harvest of their own?
- How might you use your success to glorify God?

QUESTIONS FOR WINTER—NECESSARY ENDINGS

- What in your life is no longer fulfilling its original purpose?
- What are you refusing to release that is holding you back?
- What are other people (or data) saying about this program's lifespan?
- What will you gain by letting go of this job/project/relationship? What will you lose if you let it go?
- What are you afraid of?
- How will you and others be affected if you keep doing things as you always have?

OBSERVATIONS

We have helped many people transition through various seasons. Here are some further observations:

- Four friends of the same age can meet for lunch and discover that they are each experiencing a different season. Seasons are not generally age-related.

- People can often detect changing seasons in someone else's life more easily than in their own.

- Husbands and wives may not be in the same season as each other. The husband could be experiencing a harvest while his wife undergoes a winter.

- Transitions often determine whether people thrive in the next season.

- Beginnings are typically easier to manage than endings. People should regularly take stock of what relationships, jobs, habits, or responsibilities they should release.

- Sometimes people refuse to let go of something until the pain becomes intolerable. Having someone ask hard questions before it is too late is invaluable.

- Transitioning to a new season does not mean the previous season was bad. It might have been highly enjoyable and prosperous. But a person should not cling to any season past its expiry date.

- People cannot "redo" a season. They can only embrace the next one and resolve to handle it better than the previous one!

- Some people are addicted to the excitement of spring, but they are not disciplined enough to persevere through the hard work of summer. They need someone to encourage them to finish well.
- People can experience multiple seasons at once. For example, a woman might experience winter as her husband is killed in a traffic accident, while simultaneously entering spring at her new job. But one season is typically dominant. Careers and family relationships often determine a person's season of life.
- Even 90-year-olds can experience new springs. Fruitful saints never stop learning and growing.
- Winter doesn't have to last long if people allow it to accomplish its purpose.

CONCLUSION

Seasons require transitions, and people do not always handle them well. They often resist change or are surprised when it comes. Coaches can help people recognize and embrace their current season. Coaches are most helpful when they are properly dealing with the changing seasons in their own life.

FOR REFLECTION AND DISCUSSION

1. In what areas of your life are you currently experiencing
   - Spring—a time of beginnings.
   - Summer—a time of maturing and labor.

- Autumn—a time of harvest.
- Winter—a time of endings.

2. Which season have you struggled with the most? Which have you enjoyed the most?

3. What might God be stirring up in your heart during your current season?

4. What is the next right step you should take? Are you resisting or embracing your current season?

5. How might a difficulty you are experiencing with someone stem from the changing life seasons each of you is experiencing?

CHAPTER 20

Six Necessary Comforts for Effective Spiritual Coaching

The capacity to learn is a gift; the ability to learn is a skill; and the willingness to learn is a choice.
Brian Herbert

Comfort zones are most often expanded through discomfort.
Peter McWilliams

People often ask us whether a person must possess a certain personality type to be an effective coach or if anyone can succeed in the role. Through the years, we have seen people with a wide range of personality styles excel as coaches. Nevertheless, certain relational practices can greatly enhance a coach's effectiveness. We call these "comforts." Some people exhibit them naturally; others must work to develop them. The following six comforts are essential components in successful coaching encounters.

SIX NECESSARY COMFORTS FOR EFFECTIVE COACHING

1. Not having (or giving) all the answers

Some coaches wrongly assume they should offer a solution for every problem. As a result, they tend to talk too much. Wise coaches understand that asking a well-placed question—rather than offering a stock answer—is a more effective means of sparking lasting change. Jesus often asked questions that exposed a person's heart condition. In Luke 10:25-29, Jesus replied to a religious leader's query with one of His own:

> *Then an expert in the law stood up to test him, saying, "Teacher, what must I do to inherit eternal life?"*
> *"What is written in the law?" He asked him. "How do you read it?"*

Jesus could have easily answered the man's question—He knew He was the source of eternal life. But he chose to ask a question that enabled the man to reach his own conclusion.

Coaches should patiently allow the coachee to journey toward the answer. As a result, the client will experience God's solution rather than the coach's opinion.

2. Creative Silence

Coaches should feel comfortable allowing and maintaining silence during a coaching session. God indicated that people could find His answers in repentance, rest, quietness, and trust. Yet people often feel compelled to flood silent moments with unnecessary chatter. God's Word spoken through Isaiah addresses the inner resistance both coach and client may feel toward silence: *"In repentance and rest is your salvation, in quietness and trust is your strength, but you would have none of it"* (Is. 30:15). If people are not careful, the mundane sounds of everyday life can prevent God's voice from penetrating their soul.

During a doctoral seminar on spiritual formation, my (Bob) professor instructed the class to spend several hours silently reflecting on God's presence. Since one of my classmates was a newcomer to the Pacific Northwest, we decided to commence our silent retreat while driving to the beautiful Oregon coast together. As I struggled not to speak, explain myself, or act as a tour guide for my friend, I learned a powerful lesson about my compulsive need to communicate.

If a client does not respond to a question immediately, coaches may fear it was ineffective. They might be tempted to clarify their meaning or—even worse— repeat themselves. But silence is not always bad. Coaches should allow space in the conversation for the Holy Spirit to enter into His own dialogue with the person.

If significant time passes without a response, the coach may need to add a follow-up question, such as, "You seem to be having difficulty answering my last question. What are you thinking?" or "What is stirring within you as you think about that question?" But coaches should not rush to rescue someone from silence. The Holy Spirit might be working to bring an insight to the surface of the person's awareness.

3. Patience with Ambiguity

Coaches should be comfortable with ambiguity. In coaching, ambiguity pertains to the coach's willingness to create imaginative space within the conversation. The coaching process is often messy. People do not typically discover deep insights in a systematic or predictable manner. For coaches who prefer order and quick answers, tolerating ambiguity can be difficult. They might become impatient as clients grapple to find answers. But coaches should not feel compelled to tie up every loose end! Instead, they should trust God's timing and the Holy Spirit's work in the person's life.

Wise coaches act as trail guides on the road to personal discovery, remaining patient as the traveler traverses new ground. Even if the guides have walked the path hundreds of times, they have never seen it from the new traveler's perspective. When her clients ask for advice, master coach Sarah Smith responds this way: "I have a great deal of varied life experiences. But the one experience I don't have is in being you!"[1] Coaches cannot make decisions for their clients. People are ultimately responsible for their own actions.

---

[1] To learn more about Sara Smith, go to: http://smithleadershipcoaching.com/sara-smith.html

I (Bob) have a confession to make. My wife, Teresa, and I tried to dance at our wedding but failed comically. We could not remain in step with each other or the music. To this day we laugh about how badly—and publicly— we embarrassed ourselves! We simply were not in sync. After taking lessons on three separate occasions we have improved somewhat, but we will never win any dance competitions!

Coaching is a three-way dance involving the coach, the client, and the Holy Spirit. All three participants must remain in sync for the insight-to-action process to function properly. Some people are simply too inflexible to adjust to God's movements. They find comfort in structures, routines, and processes.

Jesus rattled Nicodemus, a religious leader, out of his routines and paradigms when He told him he must be born again. Jesus described new life this way: *"The wind blows where it pleases, and you hear its sound, but you don't know where it comes from or where it is going. So it is with everyone born of the Spirit"* (John 3:8). Such talk appeared illogical to the distinguished Pharisee, yet Jesus' words contained the key to abundant life.

Coaches must recognize and respond to the Holy Spirit's lead. His skilled and fluid motions can be dizzying at times, leaving both coach and client breathless. But He is constantly in control and He always has a destination in mind.

One final note. Coaches must learn to match their client's pace. If the person is slowly grasping an insight, an impatient coach might be tempted to rush the process. Or if the person is experiencing breakthroughs, an ambitious coach may attempt to cover too much ground in one session. But coaches who are in tune with their client's pace know when to say, "We have made great progress today! We can pick it up here next time."

4. Balancing Grace and Truth

Coaches often struggle to strike a balance between grace and truth. John 1:14 says this of Jesus: *"The Word became flesh and dwelt among us. We observed His glory, the glory as the one and only Son from the Father, full of grace and truth."* Jesus was the only human to exhibit both grace and truth fully. Most people lean toward one extreme. Some coaches naturally gravitate toward truth telling. They feel compelled to speak bluntly. Others prefer to offer grace.

The conflict between Paul and Barnabas after John Mark's desertion illustrates both ends of this spectrum (Acts 15:36-41). To Paul, Mark's behavior was inexcusable. In the apostle's opinion, too much was at stake to give a former deserter a second chance. Barnabas, on the other hand, exhibited grace. Just as he had trusted Paul when no one else had, Barnabas believed John Mark deserved another opportunity. Who was right? They both were! But they viewed Mark from opposite extremes of truth and grace.

I (Richard) lean toward truth telling. A *lot* of truth telling! I often feel compelled to speak candidly with people. When someone responds well to my words, I am tempted to offer another strong measure of truth. But hearing the truth is often difficult. I must be sensitive to people's pain threshold. Conversely, too much grace might lead some people to become complacent. Spirit-sensitive coaches can determine what measure of grace and truth their client requires in each encounter.

5. Calling for Commitment

Like a frightened child standing at the edge of a swimming pool, people are often reluctant to make commitments. Excuses include timing (e.g., I'll do it later), circumstances (e.g., I'll do it after my car is paid off), spiritual rationales (e.g., I'll pray about it some more), and relational pretexts (e.g., I will wait for the other person to act first). While each of these justifications may be valid, they are often merely excuses. Coaches must help their clients recognize when it is time to jump into the pool! Doing so takes bravery, but God emboldens those who seek Him. Some coaches offer a listening ear and plenty of empathy, but they are uncomfortable calling for commitment. Such coaches will only achieve negligible to mediocre results. Good coaching always leads to action.

6. Being attentive to the person, voice, and activity of God

Spiritual leadership coaches should recognize that three persons participate in each coaching encounter: the coach, the coachee, and the Holy Spirit. Sadly, many Christian coaches are uncomfortable with God's active participation in the coaching process. They might believe in His presence intellectually, but they do not know how to interact with Him practically. As a result, their questions may be people-centered (e.g., What do you think you should do?) rather than God-centered (e.g., What do you sense God is leading you to do?). Spiritual leadership coaches must learn to tune their spiritual antenna to God, for they cannot achieve lasting fruit apart from Him (John 15:5).

When coaches are uncomfortable with the Spirit's promptings, the success of the encounter hinges on their ability and insights. But when coaches are attuned to the Holy Spirit's guidance, almighty God directs the conversation. Effective coaches help clients connect the spiritual dots between what they are experiencing and God's activity in their life. Nothing is more exciting or rewarding than walking in step with God as He works in someone's life!

CONCLUSION

Not everyone is equipped to be a spiritual leadership coach. Successful coaches possess—either innately or through conscious effort—certain comforts that predispose them to recognizing and joining the Holy Spirit's work in a person's life. In the final chapter, we'll see that coaches must not only embrace certain comforts, they must also avoid coaching pitfalls.

FOR PRAYER AND DISCUSSION

1. Which of these six comforts comes to you most easily? How?
2. Which one is most difficult? Why?
3. For each of these comforts, think of someone who manages this aspect particularly well. What can you learn from that person?

CHAPTER 21

Ten Pitfalls Coaches Must Avoid

The past sharpens perspective, warns against pitfalls,
and helps to point the way.
Dwight D. Eisenhower

Kindness and intelligence don't always deliver us from
the pitfalls and traps: there are always failures of love,
of will, of imagination. There is no way to take the
danger out of human relationships.
Barbara Grizzuti Harrison

I(Bob) learned an enduring life lesson during my time as an architecture student in college. I loved to design buildings and was thrilled when my drawings were selected for critique in class. During the "jury" process, professors asked questions about my design, and I was given an opportunity to defend it in front of my classmates. At that time, I was too proud of my talents.

During my sophomore year, the architecture school held a competition. The applicant who submitted the best design for an on-campus pavilion would receive a cash prize, something this broke West Texas boy desperately needed! I threw my full energies into winning that contest. I knew my creative and daring design would wow my professors. Unfortunately, I did not know what a pavilion was. I assumed it was an enclosed building. Boy was I wrong! Pavilions are typically open-air enclosures, which was no doubt what the judges expected. I did not win the prize.

Several common mistakes born of ignorance have derailed or limited many coaches' effectiveness. Here are ten pitfalls coaches must avoid:

1. *Breaking confidences.* Trust is an essential element in any successful coaching relationship. One of the quickest ways to shatter trust is to divulge confidential information from a coaching conversation. Such a betrayal leaves clients feeling vulnerable, guarded, and suspicious. They might even terminate the coaching relationship. Coaches should not even disclose their clients' names. Coaches may feel tempted to "advertise" that well-known leaders are using their services. But they should strive to be completely above reproach in the way they handle people's privacy. I (Bob) clarify in the initial coaching agreement that I only break confidentiality if I perceive clients to be a danger to themselves or others.

2. *Being the Bible answer guru.* People who fall into this trap believe a vigorously stated Bible passage can solve any problem. Little do they realize that the Pharisees were the Bible experts of their day, spouting numerous quotes from Moses' law with few positive results. Jesus gave this scathing critique of such people:

> *You pore over the Scriptures because you think you have eternal life in them, and yet they testify about me. But you are not willing to come to me so that you may have life* (John 5:39-40).

Scripture works powerfully when it is shared under the Holy Spirit's guidance. But lobbing ill-fitting Bible verses at a client may cause more harm than good. Scripture has the power to transform lives, but it often needs to be explained and properly applied. Simply rattling off a series of verses can leave the listener feeling confused or condemned. Applying Scripture in a gracious, understanding, loving manner, however, sets people free (John 8:32).

3. *Prayerless practioners.* I (Bob) receive a dozen emails per week from fellow coaches who claim to possess the secret to enlisting clients. I confess, I have wondered at times how coaches who have amassed such a vast array of clients could possibly have time to help me! One such coach ruefully

admitted to me that while he teaches others how to build their clientele, he struggles to do so himself. The same irony applies to spiritual coaches who seek to effect deep spiritual change in others while living a prayerless, spiritually dry existence themselves. Jesus said, *"Remain in me, and I in you. Just as a branch is unable to produce fruit by itself unless it remains on the vine, neither can you unless you remain in me"* (Jn. 15:4). Spiritual leadership coaches must begin their ministry on their knees, surrendering to God and interceding for their clients. Why? Because only God can produce true spiritual fruit. Clients ought to be assured that their coach regularly communes with God and prays for them. Hypocritical, prayerless coaches are powerless coaches.

4. *Passive Listeners.* Coaches who nod occasionally but do nothing to challenge false beliefs are not listening effectively. Active listening creates opportunities to ask probing questions, spark insights, and identify actions that would propel the client forward. Spiritual leadership coaches can only discover the most fruitful line of questioning through active, perceptive, Spirit-led listening. Such listening requires sensitivity not only to the client but also to the Holy Spirit. Careless, distracted coaches miss key opportunities to inspire life change in clients.

5. *Skills without character.* We have heard many tragic stories of well-known, gifted individuals who misused funds, manipulated others, or maintained a secret, immoral life. These people did not have the character to match their ability, and their sinful actions shipwrecked lives, devastated churches, and disillusioned followers. Jesus likened the spiritually bankrupt religious leaders of his day to white-washed tombs—externally attractive, but filled with rotting corpses (Matt. 23:27-28). Coaches must strive to reflect Jesus' heart and character. Words are more powerful when they are buttressed with a sterling character. A person's *identity* impacts others more deeply than does their *message.*

6. *Boundaryless coaching.* People who have properly aligned priorities attract others. In their desperate search for clients, however, coaches might be tempted to be "all things to all people," wrongly reasoning that making themselves available at all hours enhances their credibility. The opposite is often true. Coaches must learn to say "no" to certain activities so they can give a clear and resounding "yes" to pursuits that fit their focus, training, and skills. Coaches should contemplate questions such as these when determining which clients to accept:

   • What kind of coaching best fits my passions, calling, and giftedness? Consider the words of Frederick Buechner, "Your vocation in life is where your greatest joy meets the world's greatest need."

- What would I *not* do to land a client or win over my child? If the list is empty, trouble and heartache await.
- How will I ensure that no relational or sexual boundaries are crossed? Some coaches, for example, only coach individuals of the same gender, while others put clear boundaries in place (such as only coaching in public places, avoiding physical touch, etc.) and clearly communicate those boundaries to clients.
- Am I only coaching someone for personal gain (e.g., remuneration)? If I am not seeing genuine progress, should I refer the client to someone who is better suited to help?

7. *Shade-tree psychologists.* Coaches inevitably experience problems when they veer outside the boundaries of their skills and training. A coach is not a psychologist, for example, and should not pretend to be one. Coaching works best with people who are in a position to reflect on their situation, take steps forward, and overcome challenges. If someone is not healthy enough to engage in fruitful coaching, the coach may need to refer the person to an appropriate professional. Coaches harm others when they overestimate their abilities.

8. *Self-focused coaches.* If the most important person in the room is the coach, the exchange is not about coaching but self-promotion. Effective coaches are client-centered. They should not match every one of their client's experiences with one of their own. They should not do the majority of the talking, and they certainly should not focus on their own problems or concerns while helping a client. Their focus, prayers, questions, and observations should bring out God's best in their clients. If the client leaves the session marveling at the coach's knowledge, the coach has failed. If the client leaves the meeting with fresh insights from God, the encounter was effective.

9. *Confronter-in-chief.* When I (Bob) was a young college student, I felt deeply convicted about my sinfulness. What did I do? In my youthful, guilt-fueled enthusiasm, I confronted my cousin and pointed out the ways I believed *he* needed to change! For a while, my advice appeared to produce desirable results. Eventually, however, he turned away from both God and me. I have long regretted that my actions, motivated by my own projected shame, caused someone I cared about to question God's love.

Frequent confrontation blocks rather than encourages an intimate relationship with God. Quite frankly, it is extremely difficult to be both combative and humble at the same time. Should coaches ever confront people? Certainly! But a love of confrontation is a tumor within the coach's heart that should be excised immediately. Otherwise, the coach's efforts will produce bitter fruit rather than freedom. While coaches must share bold truths at times, they should always do so with an ample seasoning of grace. Simply identifying a person's problems or shortcomings does not solve any problems. Coaches must encourage clients to take positive steps toward a solution.

10. *Coaching the problem, not the person.* Many church-goers have encountered Bible study teachers who deliver lessons without meaningfully engaging the listeners: no eye contact, no discussion, no application to everyday life. Coaches fall into the same trap when they become so fixated on solving the problem that they neglect the client. Such coaches can run roughshod over their client in an effort to find a solution. Instead, effective coaches keep the client as their central focus. What motivates her? What limiting beliefs are holding him back? What hidden strengths does she possess? How does he need to be encouraged? Coaches empower people to solve their own problems.

CONCLUSION

The apostle James warned that not everyone should aspire to be a teacher, for teachers will receive a stricter judgment (James 3:1). Likewise, being a spiritual leadership coach is a noble calling, but not everyone is skilled, suited, or prepared for the role. Coaching someone while spiritually compromised can cause enormous harm. Coaches must guard themselves against each of these pitfalls in order to protect both themselves and their clients.

FOR REFLECTION AND DISCUSSION

1. Which pitfall most alarms or frightens you? Why?
2. Which pitfalls do you believe new coaches most commonly experience?
3. What are some safeguards you need to put in place when coaching people?
4. You might consider sharing this chapter with your spouse and/or a trusted friend and asking for their feedback.

CONCLUSION

I tell everyone I meet that I'm married because of Richard Blackaby!"

Those words initially startled me (Richard). But then the young lady told me her story. She had been stuck in a long-term relationship she believed had no future. She was frustrated, but she did not know what to do.

Apparently, God used a statement I made two years earlier at a conference to help her view her situation clearly. She finally recognized God at work in her relationship and experienced spiritual renewal. She ultimately married the young man. Two years later she thanked me for my role in changing her life.

We have seen God transform countless lives during coaching sessions. Sometimes people shed tears when they finally experience clarity. At other times, they look us in the eye with confidence as they formulate a plan to move their life onto God's agenda. People occasionally laugh in relief after God removes a heavy burden from their shoulders. Few experiences are more rewarding than being a tool God uses to impact someone's life.

We hope you have sensed the Holy Spirit stirring in your heart as you read this book. He may have prompted you to become a better Christian friend or a more effective parent. Maybe He revealed new insights that will allow your ministry to flourish. Or perhaps God is calling you to become a spiritual leadership coach and develop a full-fledged professional ministry. We feel humbled, invigorated, and deeply satisfied when God uses our words to change someone's life.

OUR VISION FOR SPIRITUAL LEADERSHIP COACHING

We believe many people will take the next step in their coaching journey by attending a Blackaby Ministries International Spiritual Leadership Coaching Workshop (or sponsoring one in their area). To learn more, visit www.blackabycoaching.org/workshop.

We are building a network of skilled Blackaby-Certified Coaches across the globe who can help marketplace and ministry leaders—as well as ordinary Christians—understand God's ways and purpose for their life.

Might you be one of them?

ABOUT THE AUTHORS

 **Dr. Richard Blackaby** is the president of Blackaby Ministries International (www. blackaby.org). He has authored or co-authored thirty-five books and speaks internationally on leadership in the church, business, and home. He regularly works with Christian CEOs of major companies in the USA and around the world, helping them align their life and business with God's agenda. Richard has also served as a pastor and a seminary president. He lives with his wife, Lisa, in Atlanta. They have three children and four grandsons.

Twitter: @richardblackaby
Facebook: Dr. Richard Blackaby
Blog: www.RichardBlackaby.com

 **Dr. Bob Royall** serves as Director of Coaching for Blackaby Ministries International. The common thread that ties together the many facets of Bob's career as a collegiate minister, seminary professor, pastor, and coach has been his passion for shaping transformational leaders. As Director of Coaching, Bob oversees all aspects of the Blackaby Ministries International coaching and coach training ministry, while also coaching executives, pastors, and teams. He teaches and speaks on coaching, spiritual

formation, leadership, change, and team-building. Bob and his wife, Teresa, live in the Atlanta area. They enjoy outdoor sports and traveling to spend time with their three children and grandchildren.

Twitter: @bobroyall
Facebook: bobroyall
LinkedIn: bobroyall
Email: b.royall@blackaby.org

 **Brett Pyle** is a transformational leadership coach and trainer for Blackaby Ministries International. He is also an award-winning Chair for Vistage Worldwide, the world's leading CEO membership organization. As a keynote speaker, Brett has impacted thousands of marketplace leaders. His groundbreaking workshop, *Your Extraordinary Why – Living a Successful Life of Significance*, is a perennial favorite with CEOs and business owners, inspiring them to cultivate deeper relationships with their consciences so they can live fulfilling lives of purpose and meaning. Brett and his wife, Jeanne, live in Greenville, SC. They have three adult children.

Twitter: @btpyle
LinkedIn: brettpyle
Email: bp@brettpyle.com
Web: www.brettpyle.com

THE DYNAMICS OF SPIRITUAL LEADERSHIP COACHING WORKSHOP

Learn 12 Essential Spiritual Leadership Coaching Skills

God has placed you in the position of "Trusted Advisor" to some key leaders around you. They seek your counsel. Some want your advice. But do you have the coaching skills to help them most effectively?

What is spiritual coaching? How does it differ from consulting or counseling?

What are the 12 essential coaching skills? How do you use them to help people move onto God's agenda?

How does dependence on the Holy Spirit fit into the coaching process?

Is the coach's role to hear from God for people or to help them hear from Him themselves?

The three-day workshop will provide an introduction to key transformational skills and principles, while also serving as the first step of the BMI Leadership Coaching Certification program.

We integrate the biblical principles found in *Experiencing God* and *Spiritual Leadership* with key coaching skills to help you become more effective at guiding the people you serve to connect with God's agenda.

- Gain a solid understanding of the Biblical role of the Spiritual Leadership Coach.
- Develop new skills to perform effectively in that role.
- Take the first step toward becoming a Blackaby-certified, Spiritual Leadership Coach.

This workshop includes:

- 18 hours of practical training
- Lunch Available each day
- Dinner, conversation, Q&A with the Blackaby's
- Course manual
- Autographed copies of Spiritual Leadership and Spiritual Leadership Coaching books

To learn more, register for, or sponsor a coaching workshop, go to www.blackabycoaching.org.

BECOME A BLACKABY-CERTIFIED COACH

A coach approach to helping people experience God and lead from His agenda.

PURPOSE

- To broaden and expand the Kingdom impact of the Experiencing God and Spiritual Leadership message through the avenue of coaching
- To equip coaches who will possess a recognized skill-set in spiritual leadership coaching
- To have a pool of effective spiritual leadership coaches for referrals
- To bring coaching into its full spiritual potential

Certificate Training Process Intent is to insure that persons certified by BMI have:

1. Fully understood the principles of Experiencing God and Spiritual Leadership
2. Are continuing to apply that message to their own lives
3. Understand the Twelve Essential Coaching Skills
4. Have practiced integrating those skills within a Spiritual Leadership Coaching context to the level of acceptable competence and commitmen

CERTIFICATE TRAINING PROCESS REQUIRED ELEMENTS

The certification process is regularly being updated. The following agenda is subject to change.

LEARN

Successful completion of The Dynamics of Spiritual Leadership Coaching Workshop

Read:

- *Experiencing God*
- *Hearing God's Voice*
- *Spiritual Leadership, Revised & Expanded*
- *Spiritual Leadership Coaching*

GROW

Spiritual Leadership Assessment Coaching Session
Three additional Coaching Sessions with a BMI Lead Coach
Thirty Days of Spiritual Journaling (see format below)

PRACTICE

Triad coaching—ten sessions, with evaluations, and ten sessions being coached (five each with two different Certification peers)
Additional coaching—fifteen sessions total coaching a minimum of at least three different persons not related to you, with evaluations Coaching sessions should be for at least one hour each.

DEMONSTRATE COMPETENCE

Live Coaching Evaluation
Spiritual Leadership Interview

COMMIT

Coach consistent with Blackaby Statement of Beliefs, Seven Realities principles, and according to the Ethical Guidelines of the International Coach Federation.

PORTFOLIO includes:

- Book Summaries and Reflections
- Spiritual Journal
- Triad Coaching Logs
- Additional Coaching Evaluations (three persons)

COST includes:

- Workshop (workshop registration applied to fee)
- Books
- Spiritual Leadership Assessment Coaching Session
- Three Additional Coaching Sessions
- Triad Placement
- Evaluation and Feedback
- Blackaby Interview
- Signed Certificate
- Website Listing
- Special training opportunities (retreats are extra)

Payment Schedule

For current pricing, see http://blackabycoaching.org/certification/

Testimony:

" When we started our church we knew we wanted to be able to 'hand-craft followers of Jesus' one person at a time and have attempted to shift away from cookie cutter programs. But, that's easier said than done. I grew up in and ministered in churches with a 'big program' and Sunday School mindset where people were mass processed in our discipleship efforts. I had a sense that there had to be a better way to come alongside people who wanted to grow and I desperately needed the framework, mindset and skills to do that effectively. I looked at a lot of discipleship programs and coaching options and I decided to add the Coaching Certification from Blackaby International to my tool box. As a pastor I have a dozen or more offers come through my inbox and mailbox monthly to sell me on a new curriculum or a better set of tools to get people into the Bible, etc. But, what I knew I needed most was life on life training in how to coach people into God's agenda for their lives. I needed to learn how to listen, use Scripture properly, how to help someone tune their hearts toward the will of God and then assist him/ her in crafting a personal plan of action. The Blackably Coach Training process is doing all that for me. I'm pumped to sit down with people in our congregation and use the tools that I've

been given through this process. I'm seeing life change all over the place and people moving onto God's agenda almost effortlessly. Thanks Bob Royall and Brett Pyle for a great season of training that has already made a huge impact on me and the people I lead."

Jeff Fuson
Founding & Lead Pastor
Phos Community Church
PhosChurch.com / JeffFuson.com

Blackaby Revitalization Ministry

If you sense God wants more for your church than what you are currently experiencing, we want to help. It may well be that you have been doing everything you know to do. But that's not enough. You need to do what GOD knows you should do! You must seek Him for those answers. We can help pastors as well as church members seek a fresh word and direction from God. Let us help you experience a fresh encounter with the risen Christ so you are prepared for the great work God wants to do through your church.

Two resources that can help are the book *Flickering Lamps: Christ and His Church* and the *Flickering Lamps DVD* set. Working in conjunction with one another, these resources will help you discover God's truths for struggling, discouraged churches.

To learn more, go to **http://www.blackaby.net/revitalization/home/** or email us at **information@blackaby.org**

DEVELOPING A POWERFUL PRAYING CHURCH

Today's Church faces challenges and crises it can only overcome through prayer. In their latest book, Developing a Powerful Praying Church, **Richard Blackaby** and **Rick Fisher** focus on the adjustments pastors and church leaders must make in their prayer life in order to see a rebirth of God-honoring, world-impacting churches across our nation.

Our hope is that God will use this book to kindle a burning desire within your soul to become a person who prays with the same depth, fervency, and faith as Jesus did when He walked on the earth. Never underestimate what God can do through a praying church!

Living Out of the Overflow

This book is written for the many Christians who have experienced "dry" periods in their life. Many Christian souls have become barren and parched due to life's trials and burdens.

The irony is that Christians have living water available within them! In the pages of "Overflow", Dr. Richard Blackaby shares a treasure trove of biblical truths that can help you experience living water each day as you abide in Christ and as you serve Him.

We invite you to walk alongside Moses and Elijah and see how they ultimately learned to live and lead out of the overflow of their personal walk with God.

As you read these pages, may you find refreshing and nourishment and be empowered to undertake God's assignment for you. God doesn't just want you to survive. He wants you to live and minister out of the overflow of His abundance.

To learn more, email us at **information@blackaby.org**

Recommendation:

Whether serving as a senior pastor, seminary president or president of Blackaby Ministries International, Richard Blackaby is a visible demonstration of what it means to be *Living Out of the Overflow*. His new book of the same title is one that should bless those who may be living minimally, yet long to live in God's abundance.

> — ANNE GRAHAM LOTZ, President and Founder of AnGeL Ministries

Apply the truths of *Experiencing God* to every area of your church

Experiencing God: Knowing and Doing the Will of God

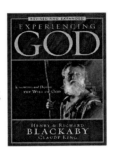

Henry Blackaby, Richard Blackaby and Claude King guide believers through seven Scriptural realities that teach us how to develop a true relationship with the Creator. By understanding how God is working through us even as we try to fathom His ways, we can begin to clearly know and do His will and discover our lives greatly and gracefully changed.

Member Book
Leader's Kit (DVDs)

Your Church Experiencing God Together

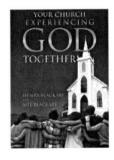

Henry and Mel Blackaby demonstrate God's plan for all believers to utilize their spiritual gifts as part of a loving church body, under Christ's headship, empowered by the Holy Spirit to become a world mission strategy center.

Member Book
DVDs

When God Speaks

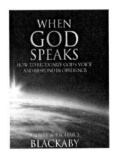

Henry and Richard Blackaby help believers to understand God does speak to His followers and that He gives clear, personal instructions that enable believers to experience fully His power, presence, and love.

Member Book

Experiencing God as Couples

Henry and Marilynn Blackaby lead married couples to experience God's presence in a way that will last a lifetime. This study has influenced thousands of lives, resulting in saved marriages, spouses coming to Jesus, rededications, couples volunteering for missions, and enriched marriages.

Member Book
DVDs

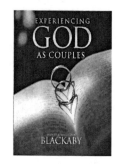

The Man God Uses: Moved from the Ordinary to the Extraordinary

Henry and Tom Blackaby provide men with a study that is designed to provide spiritual direction and encouragement. Men are being touched by God all over, and men who have encountered God need to understand what He is doing in their lives and what their lives can mean when turned over to God.

Member Book
DVDs

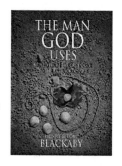

The Family God Uses: Becoming a Home of Influence

Tom and Kim Blackaby show parents how to discover where God is at work around their family and to learn how to join Him in that work. Use this resource to get and keep your family God-centered and teach your children their role in His kingdom.

Member Book

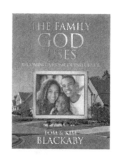

Contact us for special discounted pricing on Blackaby resources!
PO Box 1035; Jonesboro, GA 30237-1035;
phone toll free 1-877-311-2626;
email *resources@blackaby.org*, or order online at *www.blackaby.org*

Blackaby Ministries International (**www.blackaby.org**) is dedicated to helping people experience God. It has books and resources to assist Christians in the areas of experiencing God, spiritual leadership, revival, the marketplace, and the family. There are also resources for young adults and children. Please contact them at:

Facebook: Blackaby Ministries International
Twitter: @ExperiencingGod
Mobile App: Blackaby ministries int
Website: www.blackaby.org

CPSIA information can be obtained
at www.ICGtesting.com
Printed in the USA
FFOW04n2031150518
46621508-48673FF